THE JOY OF ADVENT

THE

JOY

OF

Advent

DAILY
REFLECTIONS
FROM

Pope
Francis

Diane M. Houdek

Franciscan
MEDIA
Cincinnati, Ohio

Scripture passages have been taken from *New Revised Standard Version Bible,* copyright ©1989 by the Division of Christian Education of the National Council of the Churches of Christ in the U.S.A., and used by permission. All rights reserved. Quotes from Pope Francis are © 2013–2015, Libreria Editrice Vaticana and used by permission. All rights reserved.

Cover and book design by Mark Sullivan
Cover image © Fotolia | LianeM

LIBRARY OF CONGRESS CATALOGING-IN-PUBLICATION DATA
Houdek, Diane M.
The joy of Advent : daily reflections from Pope Francis / Diane M. Houdek.
pages cm
Includes bibliographical references.
ISBN 978-1-61636-945-3 (paperback)
1. Advent—Prayers and devotions. 2. Christmas—Prayers and devotions. 3. Catholic Church—Prayers and devotions. 4. Francis, Pope, 1936- I. Francis, Pope, 1936- Homilies. Selections. English. II. Title.
BV40.H666 2015
242'.332—dc23
2015012146

ISBN 978-1-61636-945-3

Published by Franciscan Media
28 W. Liberty St.
Cincinnati, OH 45202
www.AmericanCatholic.org

Printed in the United States of America.
Printed on acid-free paper.
15 16 17 18 19 5 4 3 2 1

CONTENTS

INTRODUCTION
Pray, Give Thanks, and Help Others

*T*he season of Advent can be overlooked in the run-up to Christmas, but if we take the time to recognize its hum beneath the busyness of shopping, baking, parties, and decorations, we discover the quiet joy it can bring, those moments apart from the giddiness (or the frustration) of December. Even people who work in ministry can get caught up in the preparations for the Advent and Christmas liturgies and lose sight of the deep joy of the season. Advent challenges us to step away from the hectic activity of the world, even if only for a short time each day.

Pope Francis is the perfect guide through this season. Not one to shy away from a busy schedule, he has discovered the secret of balancing work with reflection, busyness with quiet contemplation, celebration with solitude, simplicity with the complexities of daily life. And what is at the heart of that secret? Making sure everything is rooted in Christ. The work we do (and the joy it can bring) emerges from a commitment to bringing the gift of God's love to those we meet.

Several themes emerge from the pope's preaching during the season of Advent. At the beginning of the season, he reminds us that we are on a journey, as the People of God have always been on a journey—through the desert, to the Promised Land, into exile, returning to the Promised Land, into Egypt, and back once again to the Promised Land. We journey with the prophets, with Mary and Joseph, with the Holy Family. At the end of the season, the journey of the Magi to Bethlehem and back to their own country brings us full circle. The journey each of us is on this Advent season will be different, but all our journeys have a goal in common: life in union with God.

Mary features prominently in the Advent season. Her story is our story, something that might surprise us. She brought Jesus to life as a tiny baby, giving her own flesh to the Word of God. But Pope Francis reminds us again and again that we bring that Word to life each and every day in the way we reach out to others with the love and mercy of God, the way we bring the light of Christ to a world too often shrouded in clouds and darkness, and the way we show to others a face that mirrors the face of God. During the second week of Advent, we mark in a special way the feast of the Immaculate Conception and the feast of Our Lady of Guadalupe.

The theme of family is woven throughout these reflections. For all of us, the holidays involve us with our families more intensely than perhaps any other time of the year. Family has been a strong keynote for Pope Francis. The Synod on the Family has led in some startling, even shocking directions as the Church wrestles with the many different ways people live their understanding of what it means to be a family. As a society, as a Church, as a parish, as individuals, we know the joys and the struggles of family life. As we reflect on the Holy Family during Advent and Christmas, we discover in their lives many of the same things that we experience in our own families. We learn from them and we are inspired by them to find healing and hope.

By far the most pervasive theme is joy. It's no accident that the first formal writing Pope Francis put forth was the apostolic exhortation on the Joy of the Gospel (*Evangelii Gaudium*). This theme runs throughout everything the pope says and does. The Third Sunday of Advent is known as Gaudete Sunday, so called because of the first word in the Entrance Antiphon: *Gaudete* (Rejoice)! For Pope Francis, joy is not reserved to a single Sunday but runs through the entire season, even in dark times such as the martyrdom of St. Stephen and the terrifying reign of King Herod.

He shows us how to be joyful no matter what our external circumstances might be. In this, he follows his namesake, St. Francis.

As we begin the season, we reflect on these words from the pope about the joy of Advent and Christmas. He sums up the heart of Christian joy in three actions: "Pray, give thanks, help others." If we take these words to heart and bring them to life in our everyday lives, we, too, will discover the joy of Advent, a joy that we can take with us through the new year.

> The joy of Christmas is a special joy; but it is a joy that isn't just for the day of Christmas, it is for the entire life of a Christian. It is a serene and tranquil joy, a joy that forever accompanies the Christian. Even in difficult moments, in moments of difficulty, this joy becomes peace. When he is a true Christian, the Christian never loses his peace, even in suffering. That peace is a gift from the Lord. Christian joy is a gift from the Lord.
>
> In these days, let us pray. But do not forget: let us pray, asking for the joy of Christmas. Let us give thanks to God for the good things that he has given us, above all the faith. This is a wonderful grace. Third, let us think where

I can go to bring a little relief, a little peace, to those who suffer. Pray, give thanks and help others. And like this we will arrive at the Birth of the Anointed One, the Christ, as ones anointed in grace, prayer and acts of grace and help towards others.

How to Use This Book

The season of Advent, like many seasons in the Church's liturgical cycle, varies in length from year to year depending on how many days fall between the First Sunday of Advent and December 25. Advent always has four Sundays. If Christmas Day falls on Saturday, we celebrate a full four weeks of Advent. If it falls on Monday, we have only three weeks. The last seven days before Christmas Eve (December 17–23) are set apart from the ordinary weekdays of Advent and have their own lectionary readings. One of these days will always be replaced by the Fourth Sunday of Advent.

The Joy of Advent contains enough reflections to cover the entire season of Advent in its longest form. Lectionary citations are given for each day for those who want to follow the readings at daily Mass. If you are taking this approach, you will need to switch to the Late Advent Weekdays beginning on December 17 (p. 77). Reminders appear on the appropriate pages throughout the book. Beginning on December 24, the reflections highlight Christmas Eve, Christmas Day, and several key celebrations during the Christmas season: St. Stephen, Holy Family, Mary Mother of God, and Epiphany. Because Advent is a season that leads to a greater season, we would be remiss in not taking a few days to celebrate the goal of our journey through Advent, the joyful season of the incarnation.

Each day's entry consists of the lectionary citations for that day in each of the three years of the Sunday cycle or the single year of the weekday cycle. The weekday readings during Advent remain the same every year. This is followed by a reflection from Pope Francis and suggestions for making that reflection part of your daily life ("Taking the Word to Heart" and "Bringing the Word to Life"). Using "the Word" in each of these contexts reminds us that in the birth of Jesus we celebrate "the Word made flesh" (John 1:14). The entry closes with a prayer from Pope Francis, often the conclusion to his homily for that day.

The pope's reflections are derived from daily homilies and the Angelus talks given on Sundays. Occasionally another talk or homily was the source of the reflection. Sources can be found at the back of the book (p. 119). One of the challenges in creating a book such as this is selecting a few paragraphs from a fuller, richer reflection on the readings of the day. You are encouraged to go to the Vatican website (vatican.va) to find a full listing of the various speeches and homilies given by Pope Francis since his election in March 2013.

A Journey Together toward Peace

Year A: Isaiah 2:1–5; Psalm 122:1–2, 3–4, 4–5, 6–7, 8–9;
Romans 13:11–14; Matthew 24:37–44

Year B: Isaiah 63:16b–17, 19b; 64:2–7; Psalm 80:2–3, 15–16, 18–19

Year C: Jeremiah 33:14–16; Psalm 25:4–5, 8–9, 10, 14;
1 Thessalonians 3:12 — 4:2; Luke 21:25–28, 34–36

A Word from Pope Francis

Today, on the First Sunday of Advent, we begin a new liturgical year; that is, a new journey of the People of God with Jesus Christ, our Shepherd, who guides us through history toward the fulfillment of the Kingdom of God. Therefore, this day has a special charm, it makes us experience deeply the meaning of history. We rediscover the beauty of all being on a journey: the Church, with her vocation and mission, and all humanity, peoples, civilizations, cultures, all on a journey across the paths of time.

Revelation found its fulfillment in Jesus Christ, and he, the Word made flesh, became the "Temple of the Lord": he is both guide and goal of our pilgrimage, of the pilgrimage of the entire

People of God; and in his light the other peoples may also walk toward the Kingdom of justice, toward the Kingdom of peace.

Allow me to repeat what the Prophet says; listen carefully: "They shall beat their swords into plowshares, and their spears into pruning hooks; nation shall not lift up sword against nation, neither shall they learn war any more." But when will this occur? What a beautiful day it shall be, when weapons are dismantled in order to be transformed into tools for work! What a beautiful day that shall be! And this is possible! Let us bet on hope, on the hope for peace, and it will be possible!

Taking the Word to Heart

The prophet Isaiah wrote at a time when violence and war were the order of the day. The people of Israel had been conquered by the Assyrians and would later be taken into exile. And yet Isaiah could speak of a hope rooted in the Lord's call for justice and for peace. Our own world seems to be increasingly violent. We might think that Isaiah's vision is further away than ever before. The Internet brings violence from the far corners of the world into our lives, but we also know that there is violence in our cities, our neighborhoods, and even at times in our own homes. But we also hear of hopeful and heroic actions, often by a few individuals standing in the face of darkness and offering what light they have.

The journey through Advent brings us to the Christmas celebration of God's intimate presence in human existence. What we discover is that in our waiting for Christmas, God is with us all the way along the journey. In ancient times, people traveled together for safety and support. Often they needed to set aside differences and overcome a fear of unknown traveling companions because the world outside their caravans held too many threats to travel alone. We too find that the more we try to set ourselves apart from others, the more we are threatened by a world "out there."

BRINGING THE WORD TO LIFE

Isaiah's words about swords and plowshares naturally bring to mind war, weapons, and global strife. We might think there's nothing we can do about such sweeping issues. But think about the ways in which you use words as weapons every day. How might you transform them to words of tolerance, compassion, and love? If we are to be a sign of God to all peoples, how can we behave toward people of other races, religions, or lifestyles in such a way that they will be attracted to the Word of life that motivates us?

POPE FRANCIS PRAYS

Let us prepare for Christmas,
considering that Jesus is coming.
I hope that Jesus comes into the heart of each one of you,
blesses you and gives you strength to go forward.
Pray for me! Thank you!

MONDAY OF THE FIRST WEEK OF ADVENT
A Horizon of Hope
Isaiah 2:1–5 (alternate for Year A, Isaiah 4:2–6);
Psalm 122:1–2, 3–4, 4–5, 6–7, 8–9; Matthew 8:5–11

A Word from Pope Francis

*J*ust as in each of our lives we always need to begin again, to get up again, to rediscover the meaning of the goal of our lives, so also for the great human family it is always necessary to rediscover the common horizon toward which we are journeying. The horizon of hope! This is the horizon that makes for a good journey. The season of Advent restores this horizon of hope, a hope which does not disappoint for it is founded on God's Word. A hope which does not disappoint, simply because the Lord never disappoints! He is faithful! He does not disappoint! Let us think about and feel this beauty.

The model of this spiritual disposition, of this way of being and journeying in life, is the Virgin Mary. A simple girl from the country who carries within her heart the fullness of hope in God! In her womb, God's hope took flesh, it became man, it became history: Jesus Christ. Her Magnificat is the canticle of the People of God on a journey, and of all men and women who hope in God and in the power of his mercy. Let us allow ourselves to be guided by her, she who is mother, a mamma, and knows how to guide us. Let us allow ourselves to be guided by her during this season of active waiting and watchfulness.

Taking the Word to Heart

Pregnancy might be the best image for the season of Advent. It is a time of active waiting like no other. While the people of God waited for the Messiah in an abstract sort of way, Mary experienced that waiting as an intimate, personal part of her everyday life. She knew that changes that took place in her body, the times of inevitable discomfort made bearable by the hope of all that the birth would bring. She knew that she needed to prepare not only herself but her home for the new arrival. An unborn child represents hope and potential and possibility. It is completely dependent on its mother and yet has its own life separate from the body it shares during those nine months. The mother experiences the growing life inside of her and yet knows throughout the process that the coming separation is necessary for the new life to thrive.

Bringing the Word to Life

How can you support pregnant women in a way that calms their fear and encourages the joyfulness of their waiting? Be sensitive to the many ways in which mothers-to-be approach this experience. Be willing to listen patiently on the inevitable bad days. Often practical help is most appreciated, especially if there are other little ones at home. Be mindful of the added burdens pregnancy can bring to poor women. Find out if there are local organizations that reach out to them and donate time, money, or supplies. Through it all, remember to pray for mothers-to-be and their unborn children.

Pope Francis Prays

Mary, woman of listening, open our ears;
grant us to know how to listen to the word of your Son Jesus
among the thousands of words of this world;
grant that we may listen to the reality in which we live,
to every person we encounter,
especially those who are poor, in need, in hardship.

Mary, woman of decision,
illuminate our mind and our heart,
so that we may obey, unhesitating,
the word of your Son Jesus;
give us the courage to decide,
not to let ourselves be dragged along,
letting others direct our life.

Mary, woman of action,
obtain that our hands and feet move "with haste" toward others,
to bring them the charity and love of your Son Jesus,
to bring the light of the Gospel to the world, as you did.

TUESDAY OF THE FIRST WEEK OF ADVENT
Only the Humble Understand
ISAIAH 11:1–10; PSALM 72:1, 7–8, 12–13, 17; LUKE 10:21–24

A WORD FROM POPE FRANCIS

*J*esus is the image of the Father; He is the closeness and the tenderness of the Father to us. And, the Father draws close to us in Jesus. Only those with the heart of babes are capable of receiving this revelation. Only those with a humble, meek heart, which feels the need to pray, to open up to God, to feel poor have this capacity. In a word, only those who go forth with the first beatitude: the poor in spirit.

So many can learn science, even theology. However, if they don't do this theology on their knees, humbly, that is, like babes, they can't understand a word. Perhaps they may tell us many things, but they won't understand a word. For only this poverty is capable of receiving the revelation that the Father gives through Jesus.

We cannot receive this revelation outside, outside of the world into which Jesus brings it: in humility, debasing himself. The Word was made flesh, He marginalized himself in order to bring salvation to the marginalized. When the great John the Baptist, in prison, did not understand how things were there with Jesus, because he was somewhat perplexed, he sent his disciples to ask: "John asks you: is it you or must we wait for another?" Jesus doesn't answer John's question: "I am the Son." He says instead: "Look, you have seen all of this; tell John what you have seen": in other words, that "lepers are healed, the poor receive the good news, and the outcast are found."

The grandeur of the mystery of God is known only in the mystery of Jesus, and the mystery of Jesus is really a mystery of lowering oneself, abasing oneself, humiliating oneself, and bringing salvation to the poor, to those who are destroyed by sickness, sins and difficult situations.

Taking the Word to Heart

We have more information at our fingertips than any other generation in the history of the world. If we have access to the Internet, we can study nearly any subject that can be imagined, often with the top experts in the field. With only a few keystrokes, we can read homilies from the pope in Rome almost as soon as they're delivered! But more important than this is what we do with the information we acquire. It's not enough to marvel at it, to feel inspired, and then move on to the next new thing. All the knowledge in the world isn't enough to solve the world's problems. Only compassion and action can do that. Too often acquiring knowledge leads to pride, to setting oneself apart from those who aren't "in the know." Pope Francis reminds us that the humble, who are often in need of the most basic things in life, are far more aware of their need for God.

Bringing the Word to Life

Pope Francis talks about "doing theology on our knees." Kneeling has long been a part of our liturgical tradition, and it's one of the most common positions for prayer. Sometimes we dismiss this gesture as too submissive, too weak. Take some time today to kneel in prayer. You might want to say a rosary or read the Scripture passages for today. Reflect afterward on whether it makes a difference in your attitude toward the great mystery of our relationship with God.

Pope Francis Prays

Lord,
lead us ever closer to your mystery.
Lead us on the path that you want us to take:

the path of humility,
the path of meekness,
the path of poverty,
the path of feeling ourselves sinners.
This is how you come to save us, to free us.

WEDNESDAY OF THE FIRST WEEK OF ADVENT
A Church without Joy Is Unthinkable
ISAIAH 25:6–10; PSALM 23:1–3, 3–4, 5, 6; MATTHEW 15:29–37

A WORD FROM POPE FRANCIS

*T*he human heart desires joy. We all desire joy, every family, every people aspires to happiness. But what is the joy that the Christian is called to live out and bear witness to? It is the joy that comes from the closeness of God, from his presence in our life. From the moment Jesus entered into history, with his birth in Bethlehem, humanity received the seed of the Kingdom of God, like the soil receives the seed, the promise of a future harvest. There is no need to look further! Jesus has come to bring joy to all people for all time. It is not just a hopeful joy or a joy postponed until paradise: as if here on earth we are sad but in paradise we will be filled with joy. No! It is not that, but a joy already real and tangible now, because Jesus himself is our joy, and with Jesus joy finds its home.

The word of God speaks to us today of peace and joy. Isaiah in his prophecy (11:1–10) tells us what the day of the Messiah will be like. They will be days of peace, and in the Gospel of Luke

(10:21–24), we are able to glimpse a little of Jesus' soul, of Jesus' heart. His is a joyful heart. We are not accustomed to think of Jesus smiling, or joyful. However, Jesus was full of joy. His inner joy comes precisely from this relationship with the Father in the Holy Spirit. And this is the joy he gives to us, and this joy is true peace. It is not a static, quiet, tranquil peace: Christian peace is a joyful peace, for Jesus is joyful, God is joyful.

A Church without joy is unthinkable. The joy of the Church is to announce the name of Jesus, and to proclaim: My spouse is the Lord, he is God who saves us and accompanies us.

The peace of which Isaiah speaks is a peace full of joy, a peace of praise, a peace—we might say—that is loud with praise, a peace that bears fruit in becoming a mother of new children, a peace that comes precisely from the joy of praising the Trinity, and from evangelization, of going out to people to tell them who Jesus is.

TAKING THE WORD TO HEART

Have you ever been surrounded by a whirlwind of activity, perhaps in the midst of family and friends, and felt a sudden whoosh of deep contentment? This is what Pope Francis is talking about when he refers to a "joyful peace." It's the swirling flow of a dance, the soaring notes of a symphony. Too often when we imagine peace, we think that it needs to be perfect stillness. If we're honest, we think that we might be a little bit bored with peace. When we reflect on the life of Jesus in the Gospels, we realize he was almost always in motion: walking, preaching, teaching, healing, eating, and drinking. Even when he went off to deserted places to pray, one imagines that he was in an active communion with his Father.

BRINGING THE WORD TO LIFE

As you go through the activities of your day, notice the times when you feel contentment and joy. If you find yourself feeling stressed and surrounded by chaos, take a few deep breaths and bring your attention back to Jesus. Remind yourself that he is the reason for all of this seasonal activity.

POPE FRANCIS PRAYS

Isaiah speaks of a peace full of joy,
a peace of praise,
a peace that bears fruit.
Let us pray that the Lord might give us all
this peace, this joy.

THURSDAY OF THE FIRST WEEK OF ADVENT
Don't Worry about an Umbrella
Isaiah 26:1–6; Psalm 118:1, 8–9, 19–21, 25–27a; Matthew 7:21, 24–27

A Word from Pope Francis

There are those who are Christians only in appearance: people who make themselves up as Christians, but in the moment of truth they have only makeup. And we all know what happens when a woman, all made up, gets caught in the rain without an umbrella: it all comes off, appearances wind up on the ground. That makeup is a temptation.

On the other hand, we have so many saints among the People of God, who are not necessarily canonized, but saints! So many men and women who lead their life in Christ, who put the Commandments into practice, who put Jesus' love into practice. So many!

Let's consider the smallest: the sick who offer their suffering for the Church, for others. Let's consider the many lonely elderly people who pray and offer. Let's consider the many mothers and fathers who work so hard for their family, their children's education, daily work, problems, always with hope in Jesus. They don't strut about, but rather they do what they can. Let's consider the many priests who work with such love in their parishes: catechesis for the children, care for the elderly and the sick, preparation for newlyweds. And every day it's the same, the same, the same. They don't tire because the rock is their foundation.

Jesus: this is what gives holiness to the Church; this is what gives hope. We have to take great care of the hidden holiness that there is in the Church.

Taking the Word to Heart

The Gospel image of the man who builds his house on sand instead of rock is familiar to anyone who spends time with the Gospel readings for Advent. Homilists often make comparisons to architectural disasters and the various storms and natural disasters that make the news. We can often look at this story and feel rather smug, knowing that we wouldn't be likely to make those mistakes. Pope Francis offers a different image for this reading, that of a woman whose makeup washes away in the rain. We might think about those who worry more about their clothing and appearance than about the people around them—the well-dressed person hurrying past someone who is homeless; the person who brushes past a beggar on the sidewalk to enter an exclusive restaurant; the business owner who discourages the poor from waiting for the bus inside his establishment. The pope reminds his listeners that relying on appearances rather than on an inner reality will not stand up to a divine challenge. We might say it's the difference between being good and merely looking good. It's a call to honesty and integrity, to being who we are in all circumstances and not having to hide behind a mask.

Bringing the Word to Life

Pope Francis offers several examples of people who quietly and joyfully live out their Christian vocation. You could name people in your own life who are an example to you of depending on Jesus as their rock. What qualities do you notice in such people? How might you make those qualities part of your own life? If you worry that your faith might not withstand a storm, what steps can you take to strengthen it?

Pope Francis Prays

In this season of Advent,
let us ask the Lord
that we may be firmly founded

on the rock that is Him:

He is our hope.

It's true, we are all sinners, we are all weak,

but if we place our hope in Him we can all carry on.

This is Christian joy: to know that in Him there is hope,

there is forgiveness,

there is peace,

there is joy.

FRIDAY OF THE FIRST WEEK OF ADVENT
The Bothersome Cry
ISAIAH 29:17–24; PSALM 27:1, 4, 13–14; MATTHEW 9:27–31

A WORD FROM POPE FRANCIS

Here crying aloud is a sign of prayer. Jesus himself, when he taught his disciples how to pray, told them to pray like the bothersome friend who went at midnight to ask for bread and a little pasta for his guests. Or again, he told them to do as the widow with the corrupt judge. To do so—I would say—by being bothersome. I don't know, perhaps this sounds rather bad, but praying is a little like bothering God so that he listens to us. Prayer is a matter of drawing God's eyes and heart to us.

This is how Jesus teaches us to pray. We generally bring our requests to the Lord one, two or three times, but without great strength, and then we tire of asking and we forget to ask. Yet the blind men whom Matthew describes cry aloud and do not cease crying out. In fact, Jesus tell us: "Ask!" and he also says: "Knock at the door!" and whoever knocks at the door makes noise, he disturbs, he bothers.

When we ask for something, our prayer is needy: I need this, hear me Lord! When it is true, it is also confident: listen to me, I believe you can do it, for you have promised it! True Christian prayer is founded on God's promise.

When we pray, the Lord asks us, as he asked the blind men in the day's Gospel: "Do you believe that I can do this?" This is the source of the question we must all ask ourselves: "Am I sure he can do it? Or do I pray a little but without really being sure if he can really do it?" He can do it even if we do not know when or how he will do it. This is the confidence of prayer.

Taking the Word to Heart

Sometimes we look on prayer of petition or intercession as a lesser form of prayer. Some of this attitude comes from the way we value independence and self-sufficiency. We don't want to ask for help. Or we think that it's somehow immature, even childish, to ask for what we need. Spiritual writers often encourage us to move on to prayers of thanksgiving or praise, as though that's a more sophisticated form of prayer. But anyone who has gone through great pain, through addiction, through the loss of a loved one, or any other time of trial knows that there are times when asking is all that we can manage, when our helplessness is so profound that we have no other recourse. Pope Francis reminds us that it's OK to ask, to pray to God from a position of neediness.

Bringing the Word to Life

Have you ever been unaware that a friend or family member had been going through a particularly difficult time? Ask yourself whether something in your attitude made them hesitate to ask for help. But then ask yourself how likely it is that you would have said to that person, "Don't bother me with your problems. I have enough trouble of my own." Most of us find time to listen to people who are going through tough situations. Take time today to pray for your family and friends and their needs. Listen to the Spirit moving you to offer help in some way. If you're going through a tough time, ask God for something that you truly need, confident that you will be heard. Don't be afraid to make some noise to get God's attention. And don't refuse help from those who might "overhear" your request.

POPE FRANCIS PRAYS

We present our needs truthfully to the Lord:

I am blind, Lord,

I am in need,

I have this illness,

I struggle with this sin,

I am in pain.

In this way, he hears our needs,

but he also hears us confidently asking him for help.

SATURDAY OF THE FIRST WEEK OF ADVENT
The Lord Makes Our Hope Flourish
ISAIAH 30:19–21, 23–26; PSALM 147:1–2, 3–4, 5–6;
MATTHEW 9:35 — 10:1, 6–8

A WORD FROM POPE FRANCIS

When the Lord draws near to us, he gives us hope. He refashions all things with hope. He always opens a door. In the Christian life, this hope is a true strength, it is a grace, it is a gift. When the Christian loses hope his life no longer has meaning. It is as though he were standing before a wall, faced with nothingness. But the Lord consoles us and refashions us in hope so that we might continue on.

The Lord is close to each one of us in a special way. "He will feed his flock like a shepherd, he will gather the lambs in his arms, he will carry them in his bosom, and gently lead those that are with young" (v. 11). It is the image of tenderness. The Lord consoles us with tenderness. The Lord, the great God, is not afraid of tenderness. He becomes tenderness, he becomes a baby, he makes himself little. Each one of us is very, very important to the Lord.

Taking the Word to Heart

The image of Jesus as the Good Shepherd is familiar to most Christians. Those in urban settings may have more difficulty identifying with it than those for whom sheep and shepherds are part of their way of life. But it calls forth something of care and protection in all of us. We can imagine what it must be like to wander away from the flock, to be lost and cold and out of reach of all that's familiar.

Depression is especially a problem at this time of year. The pressure to enter into holiday parties and celebrations during difficult times can make people feel as though they're on the outside looking in at a brightly lit scene of joy and festivity. The contrast makes them feel worse than they already do. Many can relate to the pope's image of "standing before a wall, faced with nothingness."

Few of us have a direct experience of God caring for us as the Good Shepherd. For most of us, that loving presence comes from the flesh-and-blood people in our lives. God reaches out to others through us just as he reached out to us through others.

BRINGING THE WORD TO LIFE

Who or what can restore your hope in difficult times? What can you do to help friends or family members at this time? Sometimes a simple gesture can be a way to break the ice: a card, a green plant, a gift of flowers. Let people know that you're there for them if they need to talk or if they just need someone to be with them in their silence. If you're the one struggling at this time, find a way to let someone help you. Trust in their presence, even if you want to fight against it.

POPE FRANCIS PRAYS

We must ask the Lord for the grace
not to be afraid of the Lord's consolation,
not to be afraid of being open,
of asking for it,
of searching for it,
for it is a consolation that gives us hope
and makes us feel the tenderness of God the Father.

SECOND SUNDAY OF ADVENT
Comfort and Joy

YEAR A: ISAIAH 11:1–10; PSALM 72:1–2, 7–8, 12–13, 17;
ROMANS 15:4–9; MATTHEW 2:1–2
YEAR B: ISAIAH 40:1–5, 9–11; PSALM 85:9–10, 11–12, 13–14;
2 PETER 3:8–14; MARK 1:1–8
YEAR C: BARUCH 5:1–9; PSALM 126:1–2, 2–3, 4–5, 6;
PHILIPPIANS 1:4–6, 8–11; LUKE 3:1–6

A WORD FROM POPE FRANCIS

Today there is need for people to be witnesses to the mercy and tenderness of God, who spurs the resigned, enlivens the disheartened, ignites the fire of hope. He ignites the fire of hope! We don't. So many situations require our comforting witness. To be joyful, comforting people. I am thinking of those who are burdened by suffering, injustice and tyranny; of those who are slaves to money, to power, to success, to worldliness. Poor dears! They have fabricated consolation, not the true comfort of the Lord! We are all called to comfort our brothers and sisters, to testify that God alone can eliminate the causes of existential and spiritual tragedies. He can do it! He is powerful!

Isaiah's message, which resounds in this second Sunday of Advent, is a salve on our wounds and an impetus to prepare with commitment the way of the Lord. Indeed, today the Prophet speaks to our hearts to tell us that God condones our sins and comforts us. If we entrust ourselves to Him with a humble and penitent heart, He will tear down the walls of evil, He will fill in the holes of our omissions, He will smooth over the bumps of arrogance and vanity, and will open the way of encounter with Him.

It is curious, but many times we are afraid of consolation, of being comforted. Or rather, we feel more secure in sorrow and desolation. Do you know why? Because in sorrow we feel almost as protagonists. However, in consolation the Holy Spirit is the protagonist! It is He who consoles us, it is He who gives us the courage to go out of ourselves. It is He who opens the door to the source of every true comfort, that is, the Father. And this is conversion.

TAKING THE WORD TO HEART

The prophets and Jesus always call us to conversion, but they do so gently. Pope Francis has shown himself to be a man deeply attuned to the suffering in the world. He has made news by reaching out to people in phone calls to offer comfort and hope.

And like all prophets, he can see through the surface comfort and success offered by the world to people who may be suffering in ways that we can't always see. It's easy to reach out to the poor, the suffering, the needy at this time of year and offer them tangible help—food, clothing, toys for children. This is the least we can do, and we will find a special kind of joy through these efforts. It can be more challenging to recognize the spiritual needs of those who seem to have it all, who aren't worrying about paying heating bills and buying presents for their children or simply putting food on the table. We fall into the trap of believing those commercials that tell us all we need to be happy is a new car or a diamond pendant.

Bringing the Word to Life

Spend some time with the Scriptures of the Advent season. Notice what words call you to conversion and what words offer comfort and joy. Participate in events offered by your parish—Lessons and Carols, Vespers, a communal reconciliation service. Invite a friend or two to join you. Let yourself be open to what a parish community has to offer, and what you have to offer to it.

POPE FRANCIS PRAYS

Please, let yourselves be comforted by the Lord, understood?
Let yourselves be comforted by the Lord!
And do not forget to pray for me.
May the Lord bless you.

MONDAY OF THE SECOND WEEK OF ADVENT
God's Loving Design
ISAIAH 35:1–10; PSALM 85:9–10, 11–12, 13–14; LUKE 5:17–26

A WORD FROM POPE FRANCIS

*F*ull of grace! This is how God saw her from the first moment of his loving design. He saw her as beautiful, full of grace. Our Mother is beautiful! Mary sustains our journey toward Christmas, for she teaches us how to live this Advent Season in expectation of the Lord. For this time of Advent is a time of waiting for the Lord, who will visit us all on the feast, but also, each one, in our own hearts. The Lord is coming! Let us wait for him!

The Gospel of St. Luke presents us with Mary, a girl from Nazareth, a small town in Galilee, on the outskirts of the Roman Empire and on the outskirts of Israel as well. A village. Yet the Lord's gaze rested on her, on this little girl from that distant village, on the one he had chosen to be the mother of his Son. In view of this motherhood, Mary was preserved from original sin, from that fracture in communion with God, with others and with creation, which deeply wounds every human being. But this fracture was healed in advance in the Mother of the One who came to free us from the slavery of sin.

And Our Lady never distanced herself from that love: throughout her life her whole being is a "yes" to that love, it is the "yes" to God. But that didn't make life easy for her! The mystery of this girl from Nazareth, who is in the heart of God, is not estranged from us. She is not there and we over here. No, we are connected. Indeed, God rests his loving gaze on every man and every woman! By name and surname. His gaze of love is on every one of us.

Let us also recognize our truest destiny, our deepest vocation: to be loved, to be transformed by love, to be transformed by the beauty of God. Let us look to her, our Mother, and allow her to look upon us, for she is our mother and she loves us so much; let us allow ourselves to be watched over by her so that we may learn how to be more humble, and also more courageous in following the Word of God; to welcome the tender embrace of her Son Jesus, an embrace that gives us life, hope and peace.

TAKING THE WORD TO HEART

The Feast of the Immaculate Conception, December 8, is one of the centerpiece feasts of the Advent season. Pope Francis points out that, like all the Marian feasts, this is about us and our call to holiness as well as something special in the life of Mary. While she was born free of original sin, we are washed clean by the sacrament of baptism. With Mary, we can say yes to God's design for our lives. In our own ways, we bring Jesus to life for the people around us if we're willing to be part of God's plan.

Bringing the Word to Life

As you reflect on your life to this point, how can you see times and places where God's hand has gently led (or pushed!) you in a new direction? How has this changed the people around you?

Pope Francis Prays

Mary our Mother,
In this time leading up to the celebration of Jesus' birth,
teach us to go against the current:
to strip ourselves,
to be humble, and giving,
to listen and be silent,
to go out of ourselves,
granting space to the beauty of God,
the source of true joy.
Pray for us, our Immaculate Mother!

TUESDAY OF THE SECOND WEEK OF ADVENT
Going Out to Give Life
ISAIAH 40:1–11; PSALM 96:1–2, 3, 10, 11–12, 13; MATTHEW 18:12–14

A WORD FROM POPE FRANCIS

The joy of the Church is to go out in search of those sheep who are lost, and to witness to that very tenderness of the shepherd who goes to look for the lost and missing sheep. Yet, this zealous shepherd can keep count like a prudent businessman. He loses one of 99, but his balance sheet still shows plenty of assets. However he has the heart of a shepherd, he goes out to search and, when he finds that one, he celebrates, he is joyful.

The joy of going out in search of faraway brothers and sisters is born in the same manner. This is the joy of the Church. It is precisely in this way that the Church becomes mother, becomes fruitful. When the Church doesn't do this, she stands still inside, she is closed within herself, even though she might be well organized. And in this manner she becomes a discouraged, anxious, sad Church; a Church who is more spinster than mother; and this Church isn't useful. Such a Church is no more than a museum.

Unfortunately we have mistrust, we are more comfortable in our things, and also more comfortable in our shortcomings, in our sins. When the comfort of the Lord arrives, it disturbs us. It's He, not we, who commands.

God's generosity cannot be transcended. You have sinned 100 times, partake 200 times of joy: this is how God's mercy is when He comes to comfort. We try to back away: "It's too much, Lord!" We so often "hire out" small consolations, but these consolations are useless. They may help but they aren't useful. In fact, what's useful to us is only what comes from the Lord, with his forgiveness and our humility. When the heart humbles itself, that comfort comes and we can be carried forth by this joy, this peace.

Taking the Word to Heart

In the Scripture readings for today, God tells the prophet Isaiah: "Give comfort to my people." And Jesus tells of a shepherd leaving his flock and going in search of a stray sheep, lost and vulnerable to wolves. The Gospel reading is one so dear to Pope Francis that his pectoral cross is an illustration of the Good Shepherd. Comforting those lost to the Church has been one of the hallmarks of his papacy. Again and again he tells us that we need to go beyond the walls of the Church, to go out into the world where people are lost in their despair and distrust. We need to meet people where they are and bring them the message of Jesus and the joy of the Gospel without insisting that they have to be perfect before they can be loved.

BRINGING THE WORD TO LIFE

When have you relied too much on "small consolations" instead of on the comfort offered by the Lord? How might you be doing that this Christmas? When have you stayed within the walls of your own particular group, away from anyone who might be different? What can you do to reach beyond such boundaries to welcome others into a more open church?

POPE FRANCIS PRAYS

Lord,
grant us the grace to be
Christians who are joyful
in the fruitfulness of Mother Church.
Save us from the danger
of falling into the attitude
of these sad, impatient, mistrustful, anxious Christians

who, in the Church, have all that is perfect, yet bear no fruit.
Console us with the comfort of
a Mother Church who goes out of herself
and with the comfort of Jesus' tenderness,
his mercy in the forgiveness of our sins.

WEDNESDAY OF THE SECOND WEEK OF ADVENT
Everything Is Grace
ISAIAH 40:25–31; PSALM 103:1–2, 3–4, 8, 10; MATTHEW 11:28–30

A WORD FROM POPE FRANCIS

The attitude of Mary of Nazareth shows us that being comes before doing, and to leave the doing to God in order to be truly as He wants us. It is He who works so many marvels in us. Mary is receptive, but not passive. Because, on the physical level, she receives the power of the Holy Spirit and then gives flesh and blood to the Son of God who forms within her.

Regarding this love, regarding this mercy, the divine grace poured into our hearts, one single thing is asked in return: unreserved giving. Not one of us can buy salvation! Salvation is a free gift of the Lord, a free gift of God that comes within us and dwells in us. As we have received freely, so are we called to give freely (cf. Mt 10:8); imitating Mary, who, immediately upon receiving the Angel's announcement, went to share the gift of her fruitfulness with her relative Elizabeth. Because if everything has been given to us, then everything must be passed on. How? By allowing that the Holy Spirit make of us a gift for others. The Spirit is a gift for us and we, by the power of the Spirit, must be a gift for others and allow the Holy Spirit to turn us into instruments of acceptance, instruments of reconciliation, instruments of forgiveness. If our life is allowed to be transformed by the grace of the Lord, for the grace of the Lord does transform us, we will not be able to keep to ourselves the light that comes from his face, but we will let it pass on to enlighten others.

TAKING THE WORD TO HEART

Pope Francis sees Mary as a guide for all Christians and especially as a role model for the Church itself. In the story of Mary going to her cousin Elizabeth, also with child, we see someone setting aside the extraordinary revelations she has just received to reach out to someone else who needs comfort and aid. Our Church has at times been somewhat closed in on itself, waiting for people to come seeking the graces it had to offer and judging the worthiness of those seekers. This shouldn't surprise us, given that the church is made up of human beings with all the weaknesses and limitations that involves. But Mary and Jesus show us again and again that it is possible to grow beyond those limitations and to reach out with divine grace to those who need it the most. Sometimes what we dislike in our institutions is something that we don't want to recognize in ourselves. As each of us grows spiritually, our communities will become more open and loving.

BRINGING THE WORD TO LIFE

Think about a time when you have set aside your own concerns to reach out to someone else who was struggling. How did you feel afterward? How did it resolve some of your own difficulties? What are you grappling with right now? What might happen if you set it aside and offer to help someone else?

POPE FRANCIS PRAYS

Mother of silence, who watches over the mystery of God,
Save us from the idolatry of the present time,
to which those who forget are condemned.
Purify the eyes of Pastors with the eye-wash of memory:
Take us back to the freshness of the origins,
for a prayerful, penitent Church.

Mother of the beauty that blossoms from faithfulness to daily
   work,
Lift us from the torpor of laziness, pettiness, and defeatism.
Clothe Pastors in the compassion that unifies, that makes whole;
   let us discover the joy of a humble, brotherly, serving Church.

Mother of tenderness who envelops us in patience and mercy,
Help us burn away the sadness, impatience and rigidity
   of those who do not know what it means to belong.
Intercede with your Son to obtain that our hands, our feet, our
   hearts be agile: let us build the Church with the Truth of love.
Mother, we shall be the People of God, pilgrims bound for the
   Kingdom. Amen.

THURSDAY OF THE SECOND WEEK OF ADVENT
God's Lullaby
ISAIAH 41:13–20; PSALM 145:1, 9, 10–11, 12–13; MATTHEW 11:11–15

A WORD FROM POPE FRANCIS

God's nearness is so great that he appears here as a mother, like a mother chatting with her child: a mother when she sings a lullaby to her child, using a childlike voice and making herself little like the child and speaking with a childlike tone, to the point of acting foolish. God does this too. This is God's tenderness. He is so close to us that He expresses himself with this tenderness, the tenderness of a mother.

This is the grace of God. When we speak of grace, we are speaking of this nearness. When one says: I am in a state of grace, I am close to the Lord or I allow the Lord to draw near me: that is grace! However, often times, in order to be certain, we want to control this grace. We often have the temptation to commodify grace, meaning to change this grace which is the closeness, the nearness of God's heart into a commodity or something controllable. We want to control grace. When we speak of grace, we are tempted to say: "I have a clean soul, I'm in grace!" This most beautiful truth of God's closeness slips into spiritual bookkeeping: "I'll do this because this will give me 300 days of grace...." With this type of reasoning, grace is reduced to a commodity.

If, in your relationship with the Lord, you don't feel that He loves you with tenderness, you are still missing something, you still don't understand what grace is, you still haven't received the grace that is this closeness. You are righteous because God has come close to you, because God caresses you, because God says these beautiful things to you with tenderness: this is our justice, this nearness of God, this tenderness, this love. And our God is so good that He runs the risk of seeming foolish to us.

Today, if you have a little time at home, pick up the Bible: Isaiah, Chapter 41, from verse 13 to 20, seven verses. Read it, in order to enter more deeply into the experience of this tenderness of God, of this God who sings to each one of us a lullaby, like a mother.

Taking the Word to Heart

Sometimes in our preparations for Christmas, we get caught up in trying to keep everything even and equal among the recipients of our gifts. And if we're not careful, we weigh the gifts we receive in a harsh balance against the gifts we give. The image of God singing us a lullaby reminds us that often we behave like toddlers during stressful holiday times. We lose sight of all that we've been given. But Pope Francis reminds us that God understands us even at those times, that God comforts and soothes us, but then sets us on our feet and shows us new ways to grow into a life of loving responsibility.

Bringing the Word to Life

Make a point this year of going beyond this kind of bookkeeping approach. Give generously in the spirit of God's gracious gifts. Let God's lullaby soothe the anxieties that keep you from living fully in his grace.

Pope Francis Prays

If we had the courage to open our heart
to this tenderness of God,
how much spiritual freedom we would have!
How much!

FRIDAY OF THE SECOND WEEK OF ADVENT
Without Fear of Freedom
ISAIAH 48:17–19; PSALM 1:1–2, 3, 4, 6; MATTHEW 11:16–19

A WORD FROM POPE FRANCIS

*J*esus always speaks fondly of children, he offers them as models of Christian life and he invites us to be like them in order to enter into the Kingdom of God. Today's Gospel passage is the only instance in which he does not speak well of them. The children are ill-mannered, malcontent, even coarse, ever refusing the invitations of the others: nothing suits them. Jesus uses this image to describe the leaders of the people, who were not open to the God's word.

They did not refuse the message, but the messenger: John came neither eating nor drinking, and they say "Behold, a glutton and a drunkard, a friend of tax collectors and sinners!" Just think of the people of that time who preferred to escape into a more elaborate religion: in moral precepts like the Pharisees, in political compromise like the Sadducees, in social revolution like the zealots, in gnostic spirituality like the Essenes. All of them had their well-cleaned, well-ordered system, but they did not accept the preacher.

That is why Jesus refreshes their memory by recalling the prophets who were persecuted and killed.

To accept the truth of revelation and not the preacher reveals a mentality that comes from a life caged in precepts, compromises, revolutionary plans, in a disincarnate spirituality. There are Christians who do not allow themselves to dance when the preacher gives them good news of joy, who do not allow themselves to cry when the preacher gives them sad news, Christians who are closed, caged, who are not free for fear of the freedom of the Holy Spirit that comes through preaching.

This is the scandal of preaching of which St Paul spoke; the scandal of preaching that ends in the scandal of the Cross. It is scandalous that God should speak to us through limited, sinful men; and it is even more scandalous that God should speak to us and save us through a man who says he is the Son of God, but ends like a criminal. These sad Christians do not believe in the Holy Spirit; they do not believe in that freedom that comes through preaching, that admonishes you, that teaches you, that even smacks you around a bit, but it is freedom which makes the Church grow.

Taking the Word to Heart

In his weekday meditations, Pope Francis is often addressing a congregation that includes more priests and religious than the average parish church! In speaking to them about their calling as preachers of God's word, though, he has a message for us as well. Sometimes a message hits a little too close to home, and we want to discredit the person who brings the message so that we don't have to hear the message itself. But God's Spirit is relentless and will always break through our defenses. And when it does, we will discover the new life that God always wants to bring to us.

Bringing the Word to Life

Think about a time when you heard a homily that "smacked you around a little bit." If you didn't heed the message at the time, what can you do now to make a change? Take time over the Christmas season to thank a priest who has brought God's word home to you in a new way.

Pope Francis Prays

Pray that we do not become sad Christians,
who rob the Holy Spirit of the freedom
of coming among us through the "scandal of preaching."

SATURDAY OF THE SECOND WEEK OF ADVENT
Our Lady of Guadalupe
ZECHARIAH 2:14–17 OR REVELATION 11:19A; 12:1–6A, 10AB/LUKE 1:26–38
OR LUKE 1:39–47

A WORD FROM POPE FRANCIS

On this Feast of Our Lady of Guadalupe, let us first of all gratefully remember her visit and maternal closeness. When she appeared to St. Juan Diego on the Hill of Tepeyac, she presented herself as the "ever perfect Holy Virgin Mary, Mother of the true God." She also hastened attentively to embrace the new American peoples, at their dramatic birth.

We can continue to praise God for the wonders He has worked in the life of the Latin American peoples. God, in his way, "has hidden these things from the wise and understanding and revealed them to the lowly and humble, to the lowly in heart" (cf. Mt 11:25). In the wonders that the Lord has fulfilled in Mary, She recognizes her Son's manner and mode of conduct in salvation history. He lifts up the humble, comes to the aid of the poor and the lowly, fills with goodness, with blessings and hope those who trust in his mercy from generation to generation, while He puts down from their thrones the wealthy, the powerful and the overbearing.

In light of the Magnificat, let us feel compelled today to ask for a grace, a wholly Christian grace, that the future of Latin America be forged by the poor and by those who suffer, by the meek, by those who hunger and thirst for righteousness, by the merciful, by the pure in heart, by the peacemakers, by those who are persecuted for the sake of Christ's name, "for theirs is the kingdom of heaven" (cf. Mt 5:1–11). May the grace be forged by those who today, are relegated to the category of slaves, of objects to be exploited or simply be rejected, by the idolatrous system of the throwaway culture.

And should we be frightened by such a bold plan or should worldly pusillanimity threaten us, may She return to speak to our heart and enable us to hear her voice, that of Mother, of Good Mother, of Great Mother: Why are you afraid? Am I not here, I, who am your Mother?

TAKING THE WORD TO HEART

Pope Francis is the first pope from outside of Europe in nearly a millennium. From the very beginning of his papacy, we have seen signs that he is opening the church to a new worldview. As he appoints more cardinals from countries in the developing world, the face of the church will continue to change in ways that reflect the great diversity of God's creation.

The feast of Our Lady of Guadalupe (December 12) is a celebration of the movement of the church outside of Europe into the indigenous cultures of the Americas. It was not unusual for missionaries to be converted to a new understanding of God's message by the people they intended to convert.

BRINGING THE WORD TO LIFE

Spend some time exploring Christmas customs from cultures other than your own. Reflect on the gifts that other cultures bring to the church. How can this make you more sensitive to issues of justice and peace? What do you find troubling about other cultures? How can Mary help you to embrace God's bold plan?

POPE FRANCIS PRAYS

Let us implore the Most Holy Virgin Mary,
as Our Lady of Guadalupe—
Mother of God, the Queen and My Lady,
"my maiden, my little one," as St. Juan Diego called her,

and with all the loving names by which
we turn to Her in popular piety—
let us pray that she continue to accompany, help and protect our
    peoples.
And may she lead by the hand all the children who go on
    pilgrimage to those lands to meet her Son, Jesus Christ, Our
    Lord, present in the Church,
in his sacramental nature, especially in the Eucharist,
present in the treasure of his Word and in his teaching,
present in the holy and faithful People of God,
present in those who are suffering and in the lowly in heart.

THIRD SUNDAY OF ADVENT
Our Joy Is Jesus Christ
YEAR A: ISAIAH 35:1–6A, 10; PSALM 146:6–7, 8–9, 9–10;
JAMES 5:7–10; MATTHEW 11:2–11
YEAR B: ISAIAH 61:1–2A, 10–11; LUKE 1:46–48, 49–50, 53–54;
1 THESSALONIANS 5:16–24; JOHN 1:6–8, 19–28
YEAR C: ZEPHANIAH 3:14–18A; PSALM 12:2–3, 4, 5–6;
PHILIPPIANS 4:4–7; LUKE 3:10–18

A WORD FROM POPE FRANCIS

*T*he joy of the Gospel is not just any joy. It consists in knowing one is welcomed and loved by God. He gives us the strength to go forward. He is always with us in order to help us to go forward. He is a God who loves us so very much, he loves us and that is why he is with us, to help us, to strengthen us, help us go forward. Courage! Always forward! Thanks to his help, we can always begin again.

The Prophet Isaiah exhorts those who have lost their way and have lost heart to entrust themselves to the faithfulness of the Lord, for his salvation will not delay in bursting into their lives. All those who have encountered Jesus along the way experience a serenity and joy in their hearts which nothing and no one can take away. Our joy is Jesus Christ, his faithful love is inexhaustible! Therefore, when a Christian becomes sad, it means that he has distanced himself from Jesus. But then we must not leave him alone! We should pray for him, and make him feel the warmth of the community.

In Him it is possible to find interior peace and the strength to face different life situations every day, even the heaviest and most difficult. No one has ever heard of a sad saint with a mournful face. This is unheard of! It would be a contradiction. The Christian's heart is filled with peace because he knows how to place his joy in the Lord even when going through the difficult moments in life. To have faith does not mean to never have difficult moments but to have the strength to face those moments knowing that we are not alone. And this is the peace that God gives to his children.

Taking the Word to Heart

Today is Gaudete Sunday. The church calls us to rejoice as Christmas nears. Pope Francis again reminds us that the hallmark of a Christian should be joy and peace, even in the midst of difficult times. We can become discouraged by the state of the world, the squabbling in our families, the economic difficulties we face, and even the dissension and scandals in our church. We need frequent reminders that God still has the world in his hands, even if we can't always see it. The world of first-century Palestine, the world into which Jesus was born, had its own conflicts and strife. But Jesus brought hope and peace to his world, and he continues to bring the same to ours. Getting back to the beginning of the life of Jesus can bring back some of the joy and innocence of childhood and remind us that a tiny faith can blossom into something much greater.

Bringing the Word to Life

If you haven't already done so, spend some time today setting up your nativity scene. Reflect on the stories of each of the characters in the story of Jesus's birth. Remind yourself of the very human details of the scene. Think about what it would be like if Jesus were born into this time, this place.

Pope Francis Prays

May the Virgin Mary
help us to hasten our steps to Bethlehem,
to encounter the Child who is born for us,
for the salvation and joy of all people.

To her the angel said: "Hail, full of grace: the Lord is with you"
(Luke 1:28).

May she obtain for us the grace to live the joy of the Gospel
in our families, at work, in the parish and everywhere.
An intimate joy, fashioned of wonder and tenderness.
The joy a mother experiences
when she looks at her newborn baby
and feels that he or she is a gift from God,
a miracle for which she can only give thanks!

MONDAY OF THE THIRD WEEK OF ADVENT
Past, Present, and Future
Numbers 24:2–7, 15–17a; Psalm 25:4–5, 6–7, 8–9; Matthew 21:23–27

A Word from Pope Francis

The prophet holds these three moments within himself: past, present and future. The past: the prophet is aware of the promise and he holds God's promise in his heart, he keeps it alive, he remembers it, he repeats it. He then looks into the present, he looks at his people and he experiences the power of the spirit to speak a word to them that will lift them up, to continue their journey toward the future. The prophet is a man of three times: the promise of the past, the contemplation of the present, the courage to point out the path toward the future.

The prophets were needed in those times in Israel's history. And the prophets were not always well received. Many times they were rejected. Jesus himself told the Pharisees that their fathers had killed the prophets because they were saying uncomfortable things, they were speaking the truth, they were recalling the

For those days in the third week that fall on December 17–23, see those dates beginning on page 77.

promises. When prophecy is absent in Israel's life, something is missing: the Lord's life is missing.

When there is no prophecy, the emphasis falls on legality; these priests went to Jesus to ask him for his legal card: "By what authority are you doing these things?" they asked him. It is as if they'd said to him: "We are in charge of the matters of the temple; as for you, by what authority do you do these things?" They did not understand the prophecies, they had forgotten the promise. They did not know how to read the signs of the present moment, they did not have eyes opened nor did they hear the word of God. They only had authority.

Perhaps the people of God who believed, who went to the temple to pray, in their hearts were mourning the fact that they didn't find the Lord. Prophecy was missing. They mourned in their hearts, asking that the people might be made fruitful with that fruitfulness that comes from the power of God, when he reawakens in us the memory of his promise and moves us toward the future with hope. This is the prophet. This is the man whose eye is opened, and who hears the words of God.

TAKING THE WORD TO HEART

The first reading from the book of Numbers tells the story of an unlikely prophet, a man whose donkey refused to go forward until Balaam spoke the words of prophecy to the people of Israel. He was not of their tribe, he was not of their faith. Yet the Spirit of God spoke of him as "the man whose eye is true…the one who hears what God says." We don't always recognize the prophets in our midst. They don't look or act the way we think a prophet should. And when we look to where we think prophets ought to be, we're disappointed to find only business as usual. Pope Francis has done a great deal to open our eyes to the unlikely prophets among us. And he has challenged those in the church who rely solely on the power of rules, regulations, and an authority that excludes rather than includes.

BRINGING THE WORD TO LIFE

If these words of Pope Francis sound a bit reminiscent of Charles Dickens, that might not be such a bad thing. Watch a favorite movie version of *A Christmas Carol* (and everyone has a favorite!) or read the original Charles Dickens novel. As you move through the past, present, and future of Ebenezer Scrooge, think about how the spirits of Christmas or the prophets might look at your own life. What can you learn from them? How might this Christmas be different?

POPE FRANCIS PRAYS

I ask the Lord for the grace
that our heart may be simple,
bright with the truth He gives us,
and this way we can be kind, forgiving,
understanding with others,
big-hearted with people, merciful.

TUESDAY OF THE THIRD WEEK OF ADVENT
They Shall Be First
ZEPHANIAH 3:1–2, 9–13; PSALM 34:2–3, 6–7, 17–18, 19, 23;
MATTHEW 21:28–32

A WORD FROM POPE FRANCIS

The three characteristics of the faithful People of God are humility, poverty and trust in the Lord. This is the path of salvation. When we see the holy People of God, who are humble, who have their treasure in the faith in the Lord, in the trust in the Lord; the humble, poor people who confide in the Lord, here we meet the saved ones, for this is the path that the Church must take.

One could ask: "But Father, what a scandal that Jesus said this, that the tax collectors, who betrayed the homeland because they collected taxes to pay the Romans. Will they really go first to the Kingdom of Heaven? And the same for the prostitutes, who are throw-away women?" And finally, "Lord, have you gone mad? We are pure, we are Catholics, we partake in communion every day, we go to Mass." They will go first if your heart is not a contrite heart. And if you have not listened to the Lord, haven't accepted correction, haven't trusted in Him, then yours is not a contrite heart.

The Lord doesn't want these hypocrites who were scandalized by what Jesus said about the tax collectors and about the prostitutes, but then secretly went to them, whether to unleash their passions or to do business. They considered themselves pure, but in reality, the Lord doesn't want them.

This judgment gives us hope when we look at our sins. Indeed, all of us, we are sinners. Every one of us is well aware of our list of sins; however, each one of us can say: "Lord, I offer You my sins, the only thing that we can offer You."

Taking the Word to Heart

One of the most difficult lessons for religious people to learn (and one we often forget and have to learn again and again) is that our righteousness is not what saves us. Only God's grace can do that. It is easier to recognize God's grace when we learn to recognize our own weakness. St. Paul knew this. The genuine saints among us know this. Paradoxically the sinners among us know this more deeply than we who consider ourselves faithful do. One of the things that often surprises the "pope watchers" in the secular media is that Pope Francis will frequently refer to his own need to grow in holiness and faithfulness and work on "defects." When we know we are sinners, we can accept the great grace of knowing that God will save us.

BRINGING THE WORD TO LIFE

The stress of the season can often make very clear to us where our weak points, our stress fractures lie. The next time you find yourself yelling at a driver on the road or losing patience with a child or a coworker, ask yourself what you might see in them that reminds you of something you would rather not see in yourself.

POPE FRANCIS PRAYS

Lord, these are my sins,
they aren't this man's or that woman's…. They're mine.
You take them. This way I'll be saved.
When we are able to do this,
we will be that beautiful people
the humble and poor people
who trust in the name of the Lord.

WEDNESDAY OF THE THIRD WEEK OF ADVENT
When Silence Is Music
ISAIAH 45:6–8, 18, 21–25; PSALM 85:9–10, 11–12, 13–14; LUKE 7:18–23

A WORD FROM POPE FRANCIS

How does the Lord speak to us? Perhaps it might seem strange to hear the great God say: "I, the Lord your God, hold your right hand; it is I who say to you, 'Fear not, I will help you'" (v. 13). He is just like a father who runs to his child's side at night when he has had a bad dream and says to him: "Don't be afraid! I'm here right beside you."

I have always been struck by the Lord's encounter with Elijah, when the Lord speaks with Elijah. He was on the mountain when he saw the Lord pass by, not in the hail, in the rain, in the storm, in the wind…. The Lord was in the still soft breeze" (cf. 1 Kings 19:11–13). In the original text, a most beautiful word is used which cannot be precisely translated: he was in a sonorous thread of silence. A sonorous thread of silence: this is how the Lord draws near, with that sound of silence that belongs to love.

This is the music of the Lord's language. As we prepare for Christmas, we should listen to it. It will do us great, great good.

Normally Christmas is a loud feast, so it will do us good to be silent a little, in order to listen to these words of love, of great closeness, these words of tenderness. We need to be silent during this season so that, as the preface says, "we might vigilantly keep watch."

Taking the Word to Heart

The pope refers here to a story from the book of Kings. It's one of my favorites. Elijah, hiding from King Ahab and Queen Jezebel, finds himself feeling abandoned by the Lord. While he's in a cave on the mountain, he encounters thunder, fire, and earthquake, all traditional ways in which God was revealed to the people. But God wasn't in any of those things. After the tumult subsided, Elijah experience God in a mere whisper of a breeze. More than once during this busy season we might find ourselves wanting to run away to a deserted place. We get caught up in seeking the spirit of the season in the music, the parties, the gifts, and all the other trappings of the holidays. But Advent calls us again and again to seek God in the silence.

Bringing the Word to Life

Make a commitment to spend some time being very quiet for as much time as you can spare from your busy schedule in the next two weeks. It might be an early morning, a late night, a lunch hour in a neighborhood church, or a walk in a park or woods. Savor the silence, the peace, the retreat from the hustle and bustle of the world's celebration of the season. Notice how it makes a difference as you resume your own preparations. You might decide you want to do this more than once!

Pope Francis Prays

May Our Lady accompany us
on this path toward Christmas.
And let there be joy, joy!

THURSDAY OF THE THIRD WEEK OF ADVENT
Protection Is the Heart of the Christian Vocation
ISAIAH 54:1–10; PSALM 30:2, 4, 5–6, 11–12, 13; LUKE 7:24–30

A WORD FROM POPE FRANCIS

How does Joseph exercise his role as protector? Discreetly, humbly and silently, but with an unfailing presence and utter fidelity, even when he finds it hard to understand. From the time of his betrothal to Mary until the finding of the twelve-year-old Jesus in the Temple of Jerusalem, he is there at every moment with loving care. As the spouse of Mary, he is at her side in good times and bad, on the journey to Bethlehem for the census and in the anxious and joyful hours when she gave birth; amid the drama of the flight into Egypt and during the frantic search for their child in the Temple; and later in the day-to-day life of the home of Nazareth, in the workshop where he taught his trade to Jesus.

How does Joseph respond to his calling to be the protector of Mary, Jesus and the Church? By being constantly attentive to God, open to the signs of God's presence and receptive to God's plans, and not simply to his own. Joseph is a "protector" because he is able to hear God's voice and be guided by his will; and for this reason he is all the more sensitive to the persons entrusted to his safekeeping. He can look at things realistically, he is in touch with his surroundings, he can make truly wise decisions. In him, dear friends, we learn how to respond to God's call, readily and willingly, but we also see the core of the Christian vocation, which is Christ!

Caring, protecting, demands goodness, it calls for a certain tenderness. In the Gospels, Saint Joseph appears as a strong and courageous man, a working man, yet in his heart we see great tenderness, which is not the virtue of the weak but rather a sign of strength of spirit and a capacity for concern, for compassion, for genuine openness to others, for love. We must not be afraid of goodness, of tenderness!

Taking the Word to Heart

We don't always take time to think about St. Joseph during Advent. So much attention is focused on the Annunciation, Mary's pregnancy, her visit to Elizabeth, and the marvelous events of the birth. Joseph is often the silent one in the shadows. Pope Francis here brings him forward and holds him up as a model for all of us. In the face of the great mystery of the incarnation, we might find it easier to identify with Joseph than with Mary. We are often puzzled by the events of our life, but we go forward as best we can, trusting in the guidance God gives us through our dreams, our intuition, our love of the people in our care.

BRINGING THE WORD TO LIFE

Spend some time today thinking about your own father and grandfathers. Think about the work that they have done, the place they have had in family gatherings and celebrations. What are your Christmas memories? What qualities of St. Joseph do you recognize in them? If it was a difficult relationship or they were absent from your life, what qualities do you wish had been there? What might you do to heal those memories?

POPE FRANCIS PRAYS

Let us protect Christ in our lives,
so that we can protect others,
so that we can protect creation!
St. Joseph, pray for us.

FRIDAY OF THE THIRD WEEK OF ADVENT
A "Do Not Disturb" Sign on Our Hearts?
ISAIAH 56:1–3, 6–8; PSALM 67:2–3, 5, 7–8; JOHN 5:33–36

A WORD FROM POPE FRANCIS

Throughout the Advent Season the Church keeps watch like Mary. And watching is the virtue, the attitude, of pilgrims. We are pilgrims. Are we watching or are we closed? Are we vigilant or are we safe and secure in an inn, no longer wanting to continue on? Are we pilgrims or are we wandering?

That is why the Church invites us to pray "come!" and to open our souls in watchfulness. We are invited to perceive and understand what is happening within us, to ask if the Lord comes or does not come; if there is room for the Lord, or if there is room for celebration, for shopping, for making noise. This examination of conscience should lead us to ask ourselves: Are our souls open, as the soul of Holy Mother Church is open, and as Mary's soul was open? Or have we closed our souls and put a highly erudite note on the door saying: "Please do not disturb"?

The world does not end with us and we are not more important than the world. Therefore, with Our Lady and the Church we would do well today to call out: O Wisdom, O Key of David, O King of the Nations, Come, Come! and we would do well to repeat it many times. It is a prayer that allows us to examine if our soul communicates to others that it does not wish to be disturbed, or if instead it is an open soul, a great soul ready to receive the Lord.

Taking the Word to Heart

Pope Francis returns to his journey theme in this reflection. He reminds us that the journey is one of pilgrimage, a sacred journey to a holy time and place. Even when we begin the journey with a clear focus and intention, it can be easy to stray from the path, to wander into a byway that seems more exciting. Or we might want to stop the journey entirely and stay in our rooms, hiding under the metaphorical covers. The pope's image of a "Do Not Disturb" sign may strike a chord with us. It can be difficult to be open to the surprising things God may be asking of us. We might be at a point in our lives when we want to say, "Enough! I can't do any more." But God keeps knocking gently at those closed doors, promising that it will be worth our while to get moving again.

Bringing the Word to Life

Pope Francis's recommendation for an examination of conscience today is a good one. Sometimes the closer we get to Christmas, the easier it is to get caught up in the parties and last minute shopping. We can forget our Advent commitments from earlier in the month when there was less going on. If you haven't done so already, celebrate the sacrament of reconciliation. Check out the options at your local parish or a nearby church.

Pope Francis Prays

Our souls are waiting in anticipation
for the coming of the Lord,
open souls calling out: Come, Lord!
Over the course of these days,
the Holy Spirit moves in the heart of each one of us,
forming this prayer within us:
"Come, come!"

Editor's note: Saturday in the Third Week of Advent always falls within the days of the O Antiphons.

FOURTH SUNDAY OF ADVENT
Recognizing God's Time
YEAR A: ISAIAH 7:10–14; PSALM 24:1–2, 3–4, 5–6;
ROMANS 1:1–7; MATTHEW 1:18–24
YEAR B: 2 SAMUEL 7:1–5, 8B–12, 14A, 16; PSALM 89:2–3, 4–5, 27, 29;
ROMANS 16:25–27; LUKE 1:26–38
YEAR C: MICAH 5:1–4A; PSALM 80:2–3, 15–16, 18–19;
HEBREWS 10:5–10; LUKE 1:39–45

A WORD FROM POPE FRANCIS

*M*ary does not know by what road she must venture, what pains she must suffer, what risks she must face. But she is aware that it is the Lord asking and she entrusts herself totally to Him; she abandons herself to his love. This is the faith of Mary! Mary teaches us to seize the right moment when Jesus comes into our life and asks for a ready and generous answer.

How many times Jesus comes into our lives, and how many times he sends us an angel, and how many times we don't notice because we are so taken, immersed in our own thoughts, in our own affairs and even, in these days, in our Christmas preparations, so as not to notice Him who comes and knocks at the door of our hearts, asking for acceptance, asking for a "yes" like Mary's.

In the mystery of Christmas, at Mary's side there is the silent presence of St Joseph, as he is portrayed in every Nativity scene. Joseph was following a good plan for his life, but God was reserving another plan for him, a greater mission. He did not persist in following his own plan for his life, he did not allow bitterness to poison his soul; rather, he was ready to make himself available to the news that, in a such a bewildering way, was being presented to him. Joseph thereby became even freer and greater. By accepting himself according to God's design, Joseph fully finds himself, beyond himself.

TAKING THE WORD TO HEART

The readings for the Fourth Sunday of Advent remind us that Jesus was born into a human family. It was important that he took on our flesh and blood, but it was equally important that he took on the social relationships that both complete and complicate our lives. We can sometimes think that it would be easier to be holy apart from the people with whom we live and work. But the incarnation reminds us that God calls us to be holy in the midst of those very relationships. He calls us to be faithful even when our careful plans come to nothing, when circumstances suddenly throw our lives into chaos. What we learn from Mary and Joseph is that as long as we say yes to God, he will guide us through the darkness with a sure hand.

BRINGING THE WORD TO LIFE

This time of year we find ourselves waking in the middle of the night with an endless to-do list running through our heads. Write out some of your persistent anxieties, from the trivial to the profound. Fold up the paper and place it somewhere in or near the nativity scene in your house. Let that gesture remind you to turn your worries, your concerns, and your very life over to God's providence.

POPE FRANCIS PRAYS

Mary, the woman full of grace
who had the courage to entrust herself totally
to the Word of God;
Joseph, the faithful and just man
who chose to believe the Lord
rather than listen to the voices of doubt and human pride.

Let us entrust ourselves to the intercession
of our Mother and of St. Joseph
in order to experience a truly Christian Christmas,
free of all worldliness,
ready to welcome the Savior, God-among-us.
With them, let us walk together toward Bethlehem.

THE O ANTIPHONS

The last days of Advent are set aside to reflect on the meaning of the first Christmas, on the salvation Christ's birth brings to his time, to our time, to all time. The Gospel antiphons for these days at Mass and at Evening Prayer have come to be known as the "O antiphons." We may know them best as the verses of the ancient Advent hymn "O Come, O Come Emmanuel." They name the Christ who comes into our world to set us free.

Note: Eight days before Christmas, the Lectionary provides a separate cycle of readings for December 17–24.

DECEMBER 17
"O Wisdom": We Are Each God's Surname
GENESIS 49:2, 8–10; PSALM 72:3–4, 7–8, 17; MATTHEW 1:1–17

A WORD FROM POPE FRANCIS

God journeys with his people because he did not want to come and save us apart from history; he wanted to make history with us. It is a history wrought of holiness and sin. The list of the genealogy of Jesus is filled with saints and sinners: from Abraham and David who converted after his sin to high caliber sinners, who sinned gravely. But God made history with them all. The latter were sinners who did not know how to respond to the design God had in mind for them. Solomon, so great and intelligent, ended like a poor man who didn't even know his name. And yet God was also with him. And this is beautiful: God makes history with us.

When God wants to say who he is, he says: I am the God of Abraham, of Isaac and of Jacob. What is God's surname? We are, each one of us. He takes the name of each of us and makes it his surname: "I am the God of Abraham, of Isaac, of Jacob, of Pedro, of Marietta, of Armony, of Marisa, of Simon, of everyone." He takes his surname from us. God's surname is each one of us.

If he made history with us, if he took his surname from us, if he has left it to us to write his history, then we for our part should allow God to write our history.

TAKING THE WORD TO HEART

When people take time to examine the genealogies of Jesus given by both Matthew and Luke in their Gospels, they're sometimes shocked at the mix of holy people and sinners in Jesus's family tree. But God can work with all manner of people to bring about his plans. Men and women, names we recognize and names that are unfamiliar, key events like the Babylonian exile—all of this is summed up at the beginning of Matthew's Gospel. These might seem like dry facts or ancient history, but the more we know of God's movement through the lives of ordinary people over time, the more we recognize what he's doing in our own time.

BRINGING THE WORD TO LIFE

Many people trace their family trees. Websites such as Ancestry .com and Genealogy.com make these records accessible to people on their home computers. But the records and documents only offer bare-bones facts. The heart of the search lies in the stories that families tell about their ancestors. Spend some time recalling not only the ancestors of your bloodline but your mothers and fathers in the faith. How has God been part of your family's story? How might that story continue through you?

POPE FRANCIS PRAYS

May the Lord write your history,
and may you allow him to write it.

DECEMBER 18

"O Lord": God Makes History with His People

JEREMIAH 23:5–8; PSALM 72:1, 12–13, 18–19; MATTHEW 1:18–24

A WORD FROM POPE FRANCIS

In yesterday's liturgy, we reflected on the genealogy of Jesus. And with the Matthew 1:18–24 this reflection concludes by telling us that salvation is always in history: there is no salvation without history. Indeed, to arrive at the point we have reached today, there has been a long history, a remarkably long history which, yesterday, the Church symbolically chose to tell us in the Reading of the genealogy of Jesus: God wanted to save us in history.

History is made step by step: God makes history and we too make history. And when we make mistakes, God corrects history and leads us onward, onward, always walking with us. If this isn't clear to us, we will never understand Christmas, we'll never understand the mystery of the incarnation of the Word, never. For it's all a history of walking. Obviously, it doesn't end with Christmas, because now, the Lord is still saving us in history and walking with his people.

For God, making history with his people means walking with and putting his chosen ones to the test. Indeed, in general, his chosen ones went through dark, painful, bad times, like these that we have seen; but in the end the Lord comes. The Gospel tells us that He sends the angel.

Let us always remember to say, with trust, even in the worst of times, even in moments of illness, when we realize that we have to ask for extreme unction because there is no way out: "Lord, history did not begin with me nor will it end with me. You go on, I'm ready." And thus we place ourselves in the hands of the Lord.

TAKING THE WORD TO HEART

Today's Gospel is Matthew's version of the annunciation story, in this case telling Joseph that the seemingly scandalous events in the life of his beloved are part of God's plan from the beginning of time. We can imagine what Joseph has been going through. We've had similar trials and difficulties in our own lives. At the time, we may have longed for a sign as clear as the one Matthew describes. Pope Francis reminds us that at times such as these, we need to have a kind of desperate faith that says yes in the midst of darkness. What helps more than anything is to be immersed in the stories of the Bible, the stories of God's presence with his people.

BRINGING THE WORD TO LIFE

Think about a Christmas that was difficult for you or your family. What were the circumstances? Illness, death, military service, ordinary work can all take a toll on the expectations and anticipations of gathering together for the holidays. How was God present in the midst of this turmoil? How were you able to recognize that presence only after the event? Who was there to ease some of the pain and carry some of the burden? How might you do that for someone who is struggling this Christmas?

POPE FRANCIS PRAYS

Lord,
enable us to understand this mystery
of your journey with your people in history,
of your testing your chosen ones who take upon themselves
   the suffering, the problems,
even appearing as sinners—let's think of Jesus—in order to carry
   on with history.

DECEMBER 19

"O Flower of Jesse's Stem": The Time of Re-Creation

JUDGES 13:2–7, 24–25; PSALM 71:3–4, 5–6, 16–17; LUKE 1:5–25

A WORD FROM POPE FRANCIS

*T*oday, the word that the Church makes us reflect on, prior to Christmas, the most important word today, is barren. The liturgy presents to us these two barren women who had no children, they weren't able to have any. In the people of Israel, barrenness was borne with difficulty: one could probably say that the inability to give life was considered almost a curse, because not having children prevented the fulfillment of the Lord's commandment to fill the earth with new lives. Yet, there are many barren women in the Bible, and always for important reasons, starting with Sarah, our mother: barren but the Lord performs a miracle.

Barrenness was a bad, bad thing. And today, the Church shows us this symbol of barrenness, just before the birth of Jesus, through a woman unable to have a child. This is the sign of a humanity unable to take one more step. From barrenness the Lord is capable of reopening a new lineage, a new life: this is today's message. When humanity is exhausted, when it can no longer go onward, grace comes and the Son comes, and salvation comes. And in this way, that exhausted creation makes way for the new creation, and thus we can call it a re-creation.

We await the master, capable of recreating all things, of making things new. We await the newness of God. This re-creation is possible only with the Spirit of God. What then is the message? Let us open ourselves to the Spirit of God. We can't do it alone. It is He who is able to do things.

Taking the Word to Heart

I often find myself in the role of reminding friends and family that all of their elaborate plans for the holidays need to be kept in perspective. I tend to take a more contemplative approach to Christmas, so I find it easier than some to stay somewhat above the frenzy of preparation. It's OK to admit that you're tired. The important thing at times like this, as Pope Francis so eloquently points out, is to let God re-create you. Let God show you the way forward. No matter how barren you might feel, God will always bring about new life in ways that might surprise you. This Christmas let yourself be surprised by our God of Surprises.

BRINGING THE WORD TO LIFE

Take a look at your to-do list for the days between now and Christmas. What can you delegate? What can you eliminate? How can you refocus your attention on the things that really matter? Maybe you haven't started preparations at all. It's OK to give the hoopla a miss for a year.

POPE FRANCIS PRAYS

Let us ask the Lord, today,
looking at the Nativity scene,
for the grace of fruitfulness for the Church.
There is so much barrenness in the People of God:
the barrenness of selfishness, of power.
We need to pray that this Christmas
renders our Church open to the gift of God,
able to let herself be startled by the Holy Spirit:
a Church which has children, a Mother Church.

DECEMBER 20

"O Key of David": Mystery Doesn't Seek Publicity

ISAIAH 7:10–14; PSALM 24:1–2, 3–4, 5–6; LUKE 1:26–38

A WORD FROM POPE FRANCIS

Throughout salvation history, the overshadowing of God has always guarded mystery. The overshadowing of God accompanied his people in the desert and the whole of salvation history demonstrates that the Lord has always guarded the mystery. God's overshadowing of us in our lives helps us to discover our own mystery: our mystery of encounter with the Lord, the mystery of our life's journey with the Lord. Each of us knows how mysteriously the Lord works in his or her heart and soul. And this is the overshadowing, the power, the Holy Spirit's style, as it were, for veiling our mystery. This overshadowing in us, in our lives, is called silence. Silence is the cloud that veils the mystery of our relationship with the Lord, of our holiness and of our sins.

It is a mystery that we cannot explain. But when there is no silence in our lives, we lose the mystery, it goes away. Hence the importance of guarding the mystery with silence: this is the cloud, this is God's power in us, it is the strength of the Holy Spirit.

I think about how many times Mary remained silent, how many times she did not say what she felt in order to guard the mystery of her relationship with her Son. Mary was silent, but within her heart how many things she said to the Lord in that crucial moment in history. Likely, Mary would have thought back to the angel's words regarding her Son: "On that day you told me he would be great! You told me he would be given the throne of David his father and that he would reign for ever! But now look there" at the Cross. Mary veiled in silence the mystery which she did not understand. And through silence she allowed the mystery to grow and flourish, thus bringing great hope to all.

TAKING THE WORD TO HEART
We live in a world that demands that everything be shared at all times. Even in church circles, the expectation that people join small groups and share their experiences of prayer and of God can put a great deal of pressure on those who are more shy or introverted. Sharing too much too soon can destroy a fragile relationship, whether with another person or in a growing life of prayer. The world is not always kind in the face of deep spiritual

experience. Holding special stories close can be an important part of our spiritual lives.

Bringing the Word to Life

Spend some time in quiet contemplation of some of the precious moments in your spiritual life, times when you felt God's presence in a truly remarkable way. Trust that God will show you when and with whom you can share such things.

Pope Francis Prays

May the Lord grant us all
the grace to love silence,
to seek it out,
to have a heart guarded by the cloud of silence.
Thus the mystery growing within us shall bear much fruit.

DECEMBER 21

"O Radiant Dawn": Our Journey Moves toward Completion

SONG OF SONGS 2:8–14 OR ZEPHANIAH 3:14–18;

PSALM 33:2–3, 11–12, 20–21; LUKE 1:39–45

A WORD FROM POPE FRANCIS

*T*he biblical and Christian vision of time and history is not cyclical but linear: it is a journey that moves toward completion. A year which has passed, then, does not lead us to a reality which ends but to a reality which is being fulfilled, it is a further step toward the destination that awaits us: a destination of hope and a destination of happiness, for we shall encounter God, who is the reason for our hope and the source of our happiness.

As [the year] draws to a close, we gather up, as in a basket, the days, weeks and months we have lived in order to offer them all to the Lord. And let us courageously ask ourselves: how have we lived the time which He has given us? Have we used it primarily for ourselves, for our own interests, or have we also sought to spend it on others? How much time have we reserved for being with God, in prayer, in silence, in adoration?

The new year will be better if people do not observe it as "from afar," on a postcard, if they do not only watch life pass by "from the balcony" without becoming involved in the many human problems, in the problems of men and women, who in the end...and from the beginning, whether we like it or not, are our brothers and sisters.

Taking the Word to Heart

The mystery of the Incarnation is that God's time becomes our time and our time becomes God's time. The Christmas and New Year holidays are a special opportunity to stand apart from our everyday business for a time and reflect on the year that's soon drawing to a close and the opportunities that await us in the year to come.

Bringing the Word to Life

As you heed the pope's words about being a participant rather than an observer, choose a cause that's close to your heart and find a way to get more involved in the work being done to further that cause.

POPE FRANCIS PRAYS

Let us give thanks for all the blessings
which God has bestowed on us,
especially for his patience and his faithfulness,
which are manifest over the course of time,
but in a singular way in the fullness of time,
when "God sent forth his Son, born of woman" (Gal 4:4).
May the Mother of God teach us
to welcome God made man,
so that every year, every month, every day
may be filled with his eternal Love.
So be it!

DECEMBER 22

"O King of the Nations": This Will Be a Sign for You

1 Samuel 1:24–28; 1 Samuel 2:1, 4–5, 6–7, 8abcd; Luke 1:46–56

A Word from Pope Francis

The Child Jesus, born in Bethlehem, is the sign given by God to those who awaited salvation, and he remains forever the sign of God's tenderness and presence in our world. Today too, children are a sign. And we have to ask ourselves: Who are we, as we stand before the Child Jesus? Who are we, standing as we stand before today's children? Are we like Mary and Joseph, who welcomed Jesus and care for him with the love of a father and a mother? Or are we like Herod, who wanted to eliminate him? Are we like the shepherds, who went in haste to kneel before him in worship and offer him their humble gifts? Or are we indifferent? Are we perhaps people who use fine and pious words, yet exploit pictures of poor children in order to make money? Are we ready to be there for children, to "waste time" with them? Are we ready to listen to them, to care for them, to pray for them and with them? Or do we ignore them because we are too caught up in our own affairs?

"This will be a sign for us: you will find a child...." Perhaps that little boy or girl is crying. He is crying because he is hungry, because she is cold, because he or she wants to be picked up and held in our arms.... Today too, children are crying, they are crying a lot, and their crying challenges us. In a world which daily discards tons of food and medicine there are children, hungry and suffering from easily curable diseases, who cry out in vain. In an age which insists on the protection of minors, there is a flourishing trade in weapons which end up in the hands of child-soldiers, there is a ready market for goods produced by the slave labor of small children. Their cry is stifled: the cry of these children is stifled! They must fight, they must work, they cannot cry! But their mothers cry for them, as modern-day Rachels: they weep for their children, and they refuse to be consoled (cf. Mt 2:18).

The Child Jesus, born in Bethlehem, every child who is born and grows up in every part of our world, is a diagnostic sign indicating the state of health of our families, our communities, our nation. Such a frank and honest diagnosis can lead us to a new kind of lifestyle where our relationships are no longer marked by conflict, oppression and consumerism, but fraternity, forgiveness and reconciliation, solidarity and love.

TAKING THE WORD TO HEART

We sometimes hear the phrase, "Christmas is for the children." And in a very real way that's true. As you watch the little ones in your immediate or extended families, you know that there's little to equal the wonder and joy in their eyes as they celebrate the lights, the decorations, the gifts and the festivities. But Pope Francis reminds us that in the midst of this, we also need to be aware of those children for whom Christmas is not a charmed and magical time.

These words of Pope Francis were delivered in the city of Bethlehem during his visit to the Holy Land in June 2014. In that war-torn place, divided by nationality, religion, and centuries of strife and misunderstanding, it is hard to miss the darkness that still exists in our world, and yet it's also a place that knows how desperately we need the light of the prince of peace.

BRINGING THE WORD TO LIFE

Make sure that you spend some quality time with the precious children in your own life this Christmas. Sometimes we get so frazzled by the preparations that we become impatient with the very ones for whom we're expending so much time, energy, and money. Remember that children need our loving attention far more than they need another new toy under the tree.

POPE FRANCIS PRAYS

Mary, Mother of Jesus,
you who accepted, teach us how to accept;
you who adored, teach us how to adore;
you who followed, teach us how to follow. Amen.

DECEMBER 23
"O Emmanuel": We Want to See Your Face
MALACHI 3:1–4, 23–24; PSALM 25:4–5, 8–9, 10, 14; LUKE 1:57–66

A WORD FROM POPE FRANCIS

This week the Church is like Mary: she is awaiting a birth. The Virgin sensed within herself, in body and in soul, that the birth of her child was near. Surely in her heart she said to the baby she was carrying in her womb: "Come, I want to see your face, for they have told me you will be great!"

We accompany Our Lady in this journey of waiting. In fact, the Lord comes twice. His first coming is what we are about to commemorate, his physical birth. Then, he will come at the end of time, at the close of history. St. Bernard tells us that there is a third coming of the Lord: his coming to us each day: each day, the Lord visits his Church. He visits each one of us. And our soul also enters into this likeness: our soul comes to resemble the Church; our soul comes to resemble Mary.

Our souls are waiting in anticipation for the coming of the Lord, open souls calling out: "Come, Lord!" Over the course of these days, the Holy Spirit moves in the heart of each one of us, forming this prayer within us: "Come, come!"

Taking the Word to Heart

We might find it easier to imagine the first coming of Jesus as an infant at Nazareth than his coming to us each and every day. We know through faith his presence in the Eucharist. We may have glimmers of awareness of a divine presence with us as we move through our daily routines. As we recall the event of his birth, we might pray for the grace to see his face more frequently. The Gospels give us some clues where to look: in the poor, the homeless, the naked, the hungry, the imprisoned, the oppressed. And once we see him there, how can we not do whatever we can to serve him there? This is the grace for which we pray when we say, "Come, Lord Jesus."

Bringing the Word to Life

Recall one or more newborns in your family. If you're a parent, this won't be at all difficult! Reflect on what it was like to see the little one's face for the first time. Imagine what Mary must have thought as she gazed at the infant Jesus. Now imagine what God must think when he looks at us. Recall, too, loved ones who have been born into eternal life. Spend some time simply being grateful for all the faces of the people who have loved you and whom you have loved. Remind yourself that what you see in those faces is a reflection of the face of God.

POPE FRANCIS PRAYS

With Our Lady and the Church we call out:

O Wisdom,

O Lord,

O Flower of Jesse's Stem,

O Key of David,

O Radiant Dawn,

O King of the Nations,

O Emmanuel,

Come, Come!

Know that today the Lord comes

and tomorrow you shall behold his glory.

DECEMBER 24

On Them a Light Has Shone

6:1–2, 2–3, 11–12, 13; Titus 2:11–14; Luke 2:1–14
(Mass at Midnight)

ᴀ ᴡᴏʀᴅ ꜰʀᴏᴍ Pᴏᴘᴇ Fʀᴀɴᴄɪꜱ

walked in darkness have seen a great light" of Isaiah never ceases to touch us, especially imed in the liturgy of Christmas Night. notional or sentimental matter. It moves ep reality of what we are: a people who and within us as well—there is darkness love God and our brothers and sisters, we walk in the light; but if our heart is closed, if we are dominated by pride, deceit, self-seeking, then darkness falls within us and around us.

Jesus is Love incarnate. He is not simply a teacher of wisdom, he is not an ideal for which we strive while knowing that we are hopelessly distant from it. He is the meaning of life and history, who has pitched his tent in our midst. The shepherds were the first to see this "tent," to receive the news of Jesus' birth. They were the first because they were among the last, the outcast. And they were the first because they were awake, keeping watch in the night, guarding their flocks. The pilgrim is bound by duty to keep watch and the shepherds did just that.

The angels said to the shepherds: "Do not be afraid!" And I also repeat to all of you: Do not be afraid! Our Father is patient, he loves us, he gives us Jesus to guide us on the way which leads to the promised land. Jesus is the light who brightens the darkness. He is mercy: our Father always forgives us. He is our peace. Amen.

Taking the Word to Heart

Midnight Mass has lost some of its traditional splendor in most places. My own parish, in the heart of the inner city, has one Christmas Eve Mass at 7:00 in the evening. Many places have opted for 11:00 or even 10:00. Sometimes I miss the drama of going out just before midnight to go to church. There's a sense of keeping watch that we miss in these times of electric lights and twenty-four-hour convenience stores. And yet, as the pope reminds us, the metaphors of darkness and light are simply that. They are signs of an inner reality. We have all had times of walking in darkness, and times of seeing a great light.

Bringing the Word to Life

Pope Francis writes, "In our personal history too, there are both bright and dark moments, lights and shadows." As you watch the light of Christmas—twinkling tree lights, the soft glow of candlelight, the tasteful (or garish!) house displays—let your heart recall the lights and shadows of your life and the ways in which God's love and mercy have been present in both light and darkness.

Pope Francis Prays

Together with the shepherds,
let us pause before the Child,
let us pause in silence.
Together with them,
let us thank the Lord for having given Jesus to us,
and with them let us raise from the depths of our hearts
the praises of his fidelity:
We bless you, Lord God most high,
who lowered yourself for our sake.
You are immense, and you made yourself small;
you are rich and you made yourself poor;
you are all-powerful and you made yourself vulnerable.

DECEMBER 25: CHRISTMAS DAY
Glory to God

A WORD FROM POPE FRANCIS

I take up the song of the angels who appeared to the shepherds in Bethlehem on the night when Jesus was born. It is a song which unites heaven and earth, giving praise and glory to heaven, and the promise of peace to earth and all its people. I ask everyone to share in this song: it is a song for every man or woman who keeps watch through the night, who hopes for a better world, who cares for others while humbly seeking to do his or her duty.

Above all else, this is what Christmas bids us to do: give glory to God, for he is good, he is faithful, he is merciful. Today I voice my hope that everyone will come to know the true face of God, the Father who has given us Jesus. My hope is that everyone will feel God's closeness, live in his presence, love him and adore him. May each of us give glory to God above all by our lives, by lives spent for love of him and of all our brothers and sisters.

Dear brothers and sisters, today, in this world, in this humanity, is born the Savior, who is Christ the Lord. Let us pause before the Child of Bethlehem. Let us allow our hearts to be touched, let us not fear this. Let us not fear that our hearts be moved. We need this! Let us allow ourselves to be warmed by the tenderness of God; we need his caress. God's caresses do not harm us. They give us peace and strength. We need his caresses. God is full of love: to him be praise and glory forever! God is peace: let us ask him to help us to be peacemakers each day, in our life, in our families, in our cities and nations, in the whole world. Let us allow ourselves to be moved by God's goodness.

On this day illumined by the Gospel hope which springs from the humble stable of Bethlehem, I invoke the Christmas gift of joy and peace upon all: upon children and the elderly, upon young people and families, the poor and the marginalized. May Jesus, who was born for us, console all those afflicted by illness and suffering; may he sustain those who devote themselves to serving our brothers and sisters who are most in need. Happy Christmas to all!

Taking the Word to Heart
One of the Vatican traditions is the *Urbi et Orbi* blessing, from which today's reflection by the pope is taken. Pope Francis, as his predecessors have done, blesses the city of Rome and all the world

on Christmas Day, a sign of God's presence in our midst not only in Bethlehem two thousand years ago but each and every day. It is both a sober acknowledgment of those places and circumstances that desperately need blessing, care, and justice, as well as a celebration of the one human family on this day of family gatherings and celebrations.

Bringing the Word to Life
Wherever you gather with family and friends today, take time to bless not only your immediate family but to pray for God's peace and blessing on the whole world.

Pope Francis Prays
Dear brothers and sisters,
may the Holy Spirit today enlighten our hearts,
that we may recognize in the Infant Jesus,
born in Bethlehem of the Virgin Mary,
the salvation given by God to each one of us,
to each man and woman and to all the peoples of the earth.

May his redeeming strength
transform arms into ploughshares,
destruction into creativity,
hatred into love and tenderness.
Then we will be able to cry out with joy:
"Our eyes have seen your salvation."

DECEMBER 26—ST. STEPHEN, MARTYR
Violence Is Conquered by Love
ACTS 6:8–10; 7:54–59; MATTHEW 10:17–22

A WORD FROM POPE FRANCIS

*I*n the joyful atmosphere of Christmas, this commemoration may seem out of place. For Christmas is the celebration of life and it fills us with sentiments of serenity and peace. Why disturb the charm with the memory of such atrocious violence? In reality, from the perspective of faith, the Feast of St Stephen is in full harmony with the deeper meaning of Christmas. In martyrdom, in fact, violence is conquered by love, death by life. Jesus transforms the death of those who love him into a dawn of new life!

In the martyrdom of Stephen is the same confrontation between good and evil, between hatred and forgiveness, between meekness and violence, which culminated in the Cross of Christ. Thus, the remembrance of the first martyr immediately dispels a false image of Christmas: the fairytale, sugarcoated image, which is not in the Gospel! The liturgy brings us back to the authentic meaning of the Incarnation, by linking Bethlehem to Calvary and by reminding us that the divine salvation involved the battle against sin, it passes through the narrow door of the Cross.

Following the Gospel is certainly a demanding but beautiful, very beautiful journey, and those who follow it with faithfulness and courage receive the reward promised by the Lord to men and women of good will. As the angels sang on Christmas Day: "Peace! Peace!" This peace granted by God is capable of calming the conscience of those who, through the trials of life, are able to receive the Word of God and commit themselves to observing it with perseverance to the end (cf. Mt 10:22).

Taking the Word to Heart

St. Stephen was chosen as one of the deacons in the Acts of the Apostles. They tended to the needs of the poor, the orphans and the widows in the early Christian community. Celebrating his feast day in the midst of a season that can so often run to indulgence and even greed keeps us aware that God, not our desires, is the center of the season. The commemoration of a martyr so soon after Christmas is a sobering reminder that while God is love always and everywhere, hatred has still not been eliminated in our fallen world. But, like Jesus, like St. Stephen, we can only respond to that hatred and violence with love and forgiveness.

Bringing the Word to Life

If you've heard the Christmas carol "Good King Wenceslaus," you might recall that the saintly king and his trusty page go forth to help a needy man "on the Feast of Stephen." It's appropriate that we do something on this day to reach out to those who are most needy among us. The poor need our attention every day of the year, not just over the holidays. We might want to make a commitment today for some kind of long-term act of charity.

Pope Francis Prays

Today, brothers and sisters,
let us pray in a special way for those
who are discriminated against,
persecuted and killed for bearing witness to Christ.
If you bear this cross with love,
you have entered into the mystery of Christmas,
you are in the heart of Christ and of the Church.
St Stephen, Deacon and First Martyr,
sustain us on our daily journey,
which we hope to crown, in the end,
with the joyous assembly of Saints in Paradise.

May Mary Queen of Martyrs
help us to live Christmas
with the ardor of faith and love
which shone forth in St. Stephen
and in all of the martyrs of the Church.

SUNDAY AFTER CHRISTMAS—FEAST OF THE HOLY FAMILY
"May I; Thank You; Sorry"
SIRACH 3:2–6, 12–14; COLOSSIANS 3:12–21
OR HEBREWS 11:8, 11–12, 17–19; LUKE 2:22–40

A WORD FROM POPE FRANCIS

The message that comes from the Holy Family is first of all a message of faith. In the family life of Mary and Joseph, God is truly at the centre, and He is so in the Person of Jesus. This is why the Family of Nazareth is holy. Why? Because it is centered on Jesus. When parents and children together breathe in this climate of faith, they have an energy that allows them to face even difficult trials, as the experience of the Holy Family shows, for example, in the dramatic event of their flight to Egypt: a difficult ordeal.

The Baby Jesus with his Mother Mary and with St. Joseph are a simple but so luminous icon of the family. The light it casts is the light of mercy and salvation for all the world, the light of truth for every man, for the human family and for individual families. This light which comes from the Holy Family encourages us to offer human warmth in those family situations in which, for various reasons, peace is lacking, harmony is lacking, and forgiveness is lacking. May our concrete solidarity not diminish especially with regard to the families who are experiencing more difficult situations due to illness, unemployment, discrimination, the need to emigrate.

Today our gaze on the Holy Family lets us also be drawn into the simplicity of the life they led in Nazareth. It is an example that does our families great good, helping them increasingly to become communities of love and reconciliation, in which tenderness, mutual help, and mutual forgiveness is experienced. Let us remember the three key words for living in peace and joy in the family: "may I," "thank you" and "sorry." In our family, when we are not intrusive and ask "may I," in our family when we are not selfish and learn to say "thank you," and when in a family one realizes he has done something wrong and knows how to say "sorry," in that family there is peace and joy.

Taking the Word to Heart

Sometimes the holiday celebrations bring together too many different family members too often or for too many days on end. As we've remarked earlier in the season, family is often the first and last place that we learn to live with and love others when it's easy and when it's difficult. Jesus, Mary, and Joseph knew the struggles and hardships of life in the same way that families around the world struggle every day.

BRINGING THE WORD TO LIFE

Talk with your family (immediate or extended) about the three words the pope suggests are essential for family harmony: "may I," "thank you," and "sorry." Take some time, too, to reflect on how these words can be extended across our family of nations.

POPE FRANCIS PRAYS

Let us fervently call upon Mary Most Holy,
the Mother of Jesus and our Mother,
and St. Joseph her spouse.
Let us ask them to enlighten, comfort and guide
every family in the world,
so that they may fulfill with dignity and peace
the mission which God has entrusted to them.

JANUARY 1
Mary, Mother of God

A WORD FROM POPE FRANCIS

*I*n the first reading we find the ancient prayer of blessing which God gave to Moses to hand on to Aaron and his sons: "The Lord bless you and keep you. The Lord make his face to shine upon you, and be gracious to you. The Lord lift up his countenance upon you and give you peace" (Numbers 6:24–25). There is no more meaningful time than the beginning of a new year to hear these words of blessing: they will accompany our journey through the year opening up before us. They are words of strength, courage and hope. Not an illusory hope, based on frail human promises, or a naïve hope which presumes that the future will be better simply because it is the future. Rather, it is a hope that has its foundation precisely in God's blessing, a blessing which contains the greatest message of good wishes there can be; and this is the message which the Church brings to each of us, filled with the Lord's loving care and providential help.

The Mother of the Redeemer goes before us and continually strengthens us in faith, in our vocation and in our mission. By her example of humility and openness to God's will she helps us to transmit our faith in a joyful proclamation of the Gospel to all, without reservation. In this way our mission will be fruitful, because it is modeled on the motherhood of Mary. To her let us entrust our journey of faith, the desires of our heart, our needs and the needs of the whole world, especially of those who hunger and thirst for justice and peace, and for God.

In celebrating the Solemnity of Mary Most Holy, the Holy Mother of God, the Church reminds us that Mary, more than anyone else, received this blessing. In her the blessing finds fulfillment, for no other creature has ever seen God's face shine upon it as did Mary. She gave a human face to the eternal Word, so that all of us can contemplate him.

Taking the Word to Heart

January 1 has had many names and many identities through the years. In our secular society, of course, it is New Year's Day. In the life of the church it is the octave day of Christmas, a reminder that the greatest feasts in the liturgical year are celebrated for eight days. At one time it marked the circumcision of Jesus, the Hebrew ritual that commemorates the Mosaic covenant. The current church calendar names it as the feast of Mary, the Mother of God, recognizing Mary in the great plan of salvation. Finally, in 1967, Pope Paul VI established a World Day of Prayer for Peace on the first day of the new year.

Bringing the Word to Life

On this New Year's Day, think of the faces in your life that bring you peace and joy. Say a special prayer for those people. And on this day of prayer for world peace, ask the Lord to smile in a special way on those areas of our world that most need the light of peace to shine on them.

Pope Francis Prays

May this gentle and loving Mother
obtain for us the Lord's blessing
upon the entire human family.
On this, the World Day of Peace,
we especially implore her intercession
that the Lord may grant
peace in our day;
peace in hearts,
peace in families,
peace among the nations.

EPIPHANY
Take the Risk
ISAIAH 60:1–6; EPHESIANS 3:2–3A, 5–6; MATTHEW 2:1–12

A WORD FROM POPE FRANCIS

On the feast of the Epiphany, as we recall Jesus' manifestation to humanity in the face of a Child, may we sense the Magi at our side, as wise companions on the way. Their example helps us to lift our gaze towards the star and to follow the great desires of our heart. They teach us not to be content with a life of mediocrity, of "playing it safe," but to let ourselves be attracted always by what is good, true and beautiful, by God, who is all of this, and so much more!

And they teach us not to be deceived by appearances, by what the world considers great, wise and powerful. We must not stop at that. It is necessary to guard the faith. Today this is of vital importance: to keep the faith. We must press on further, beyond the darkness, beyond the voices that raise alarm, beyond worldliness, beyond so many forms of modernity that exist today. We must press on towards Bethlehem, where, in the simplicity of a dwelling on the outskirts, beside a mother and father full of love and of faith, there shines forth the Sun from on high, the King of the universe.

Taking the Word to Heart

We began Advent reflecting on the journey we make as pilgrims to Bethlehem. We close our reflections with not only the journey of the Magi to Bethlehem but also their journey home again to their own lands. When they inquired in Jerusalem for the newborn "King of the Jews," they rattled the power-mad King Herod and started a chain of events that led to the slaughter of countless infants. Matthew's Gospel tells us that they went home "by a different way." They heeded the words of the angel that told them not to betray the child to the king.

We are fascinated by this story because it has always held a sense of mystery, of the exotic Holy Land, in a time before the whole world was open to journalists and cameras and the World Wide Web. And even in our own day, we can still get a sense of what it must have taken for these people to travel such a long distance on the strength only of a star and their own intuition. It is the story of God's people from the call of Abraham to our own day. Like them, we walk by faith.

Bringing the Word to Life

What did the magi see in the face of the Christ Child that sent them off again in a new way, to a new life? If you had been in Bethlehem on that day, what tales would you tell when you returned home? How might you tell the story of your own encounter with the Christ? What new roads will you follow in this new year? What risks are you willing to take to share the good news?

Pope Francis Prays

By the example of the Magi,
with our little lights,
may we seek the Light
and keep the faith.
May it be so.

SOURCES

Sunday of the First Week of Advent: Angelus, 1 December 2013

Monday of the First Week of Advent: Angelus, 1 December 2013; Prayer to Mary at the conclusion of the recital of the Holy Rosary (Saint Peter's Square, 31 May 2013)

Tuesday of the First Week of Advent: Morning Meditation in the Chapel of the Domus Sancta Marthae, 2 December 2014 (by *L'Osservatore Romano*, weekly ed. in English, n. 49, 5 December 2014)

Wednesday of the First Week of Advent: Morning Meditation in the Chapel of the Domus Sancta Marthae, 3 December 2013 (by *L'Osservatore Romano*, weekly ed. in English, n. 49, 6 December 2013)

Thursday of the First Week of Advent: Morning Meditation in the Chapel of the Domus Sancta Marthae, 4 December 2014 (by *L'Osservatore Romano*, weekly ed. in English, n. 50, 12 December 2014)

Friday of the First Week of Advent: Morning Meditation in the Chapel of the Domus Sancta Marthae, 6 December 2013 (by *L'Osservatore Romano*, weekly ed. in English, n. 50, 13 December 2013)

Saturday of the First Week of Advent: Morning Meditation in the Chapel of the Domus Sancta Marthae, 10 December 2013 (by

L'Osservatore Romano, weekly ed. in English, n. 50, 13 December 2013)

Second Sunday of Advent: Angelus, 7 December 2014

Monday of the Second Week of Advent: Angelus, Feast of the Immaculate Conception, 8 December 2013

Tuesday of the Second Week of Advent: Morning Meditation in the Chapel of the Domus Sancta Marthae, 9 December 2014 (by *L'Osservatore Romano*, weekly ed. in English, n. 50, 12 December 2014)

Wednesday of the Second Week of Advent: Angelus, Feast of the Immaculate Conception, 8 December 2013; Prayer to Mary after the Profession of Faith with the Bishops of the Italian Episcopal Conference (23 May 2013)

Thursday of the Second Week: Morning Meditation in the Chapel of the Domus Sancta Marthae, 11 December 2014 (by *L'Osservatore Romano*, weekly ed. in English, n. 51, 19 December 2014)

Friday of the Second Week: Morning Meditation in the Chapel of the Domus Sancta Marthae, 13 December 2013 (by *L'Osservatore Romano*, weekly ed. in English, n. 51, 20 December 2013)

Saturday of the Second Week: Homily, Feast Our Lady of Guadalupe, 12 December 2014

Third Sunday of Advent: Angelus, 15 December 2013; 14 December 2014

Monday of the Third Week of Advent: Morning Meditation in the Chapel of the Domus Sancta Marthae, 15 December 2014 (by

L'Osservatore Romano, weekly ed. in English, n. 51, 19 December 2014); 16 December 2013 (by *L'Osservatore Romano*, weekly ed. in English, n. 51, 20 December 2013)

Tuesday of the Third Week of Advent: Morning Meditation in the Chapel of the Domus Sancta Marthae, 16 December 2014 (by *L'Osservatore Romano*, weekly ed. in English, n. 51, 19 December 2014)

Wednesday of the Third Week of Advent: Morning Meditation in the Chapel of the Domus Sancta Marthae, 12 December 2013 (by *L'Osservatore Romano*, weekly ed. in English, n. 51, 20 December 2013)

Thursday of the Third Week of Advent: Homily, Feast of St. Joseph, 19 March 2013.

Friday of the Third Week of Advent: Morning Meditation in the Chapel of the Domus Sancta Marthae,

23 December 2013 (by *L'Osservatore Romano*, weekly ed. in English, n. 1, 3 January 2014)

Fourth Sunday of Advent: Angelus, 21 December 2014

December 17: "O Wisdom," Morning Meditation in the Chapel of the Domus Sancta Marthae, 17 December 2013 (by *L'Osservatore Romano*, weekly ed. in English, n. 1, 3 January 2014)

December 18: "O Lord," Morning Meditation in the Chapel of the Domus Sancta Marthae, 18 December 2014 (by *L'Osservatore Romano*, weekly ed. in English, n. 1, 2 January 2015)

December 19: "O Flower of Jesse's Stem," Morning Meditation in the Chapel of the Domus Sancta Marthae, 19 December 2014 (by *L'Osservatore Romano*, weekly ed. in English, n. 1, 2 January 2015); 19 December 2013 (by *L'Osservatore Romano*, weekly ed. in English, n. 1, 3 January 2014)

December 20: "O Key of David," Morning Meditation in the Chapel of the Domus Sancta Marthae, 20 December 2013 (by *L'Osservatore Romano*, weekly ed. in English, n. 1, 3 January 2014)

December 21: "O Radiant Dawn," Homily, Feast of Mary, Mother of God, 31 December 2013

December 22: "O King of the Nations," Homily, Mass in Manger Square (Bethlehem) 25 May 2014

December 23: "O Emmanuel," Morning Meditation in the Chapel of the Domus Sancta Marthae, 23 December 2013 (by *L'Osservatore Romano*, weekly ed. in English, n. 1, 3 January 2014)

December 24: Urbi et Orbi Message, 25 December 2013

December 25: Midnight Mass 2014; Urbi et Orbi message of Pope Francis, Wednesday, 25 December 2013; Urbi et Orbi message of Pope Francis, 25 December 2014

December 26, Feast of St. Stephen: Angelus, 26 December 2013 and 2014

Sunday After Christmas, Feast of the Holy Family: Angelus, 28 December 2013 and 2014

January 1, Mary Mother of God: Homily, 1 January 2014
January 6, Epiphany: Homily, 1 January 2014

More inspiration from Pope Francis!

The Spirit of Saint Francis

"Some people want to know why I wished to be called Francis. For me, Francis of Assisi is the man of poverty, the man of peace, the man who loves and protects creation."

— Pope Francis, March 16, 2013

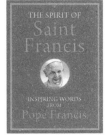

In this original collection, published in cooperation with the Vatican, the life and legacy of Saint Francis of Assisi spring to life through the pope's uplifting and challenging words. He presents an irresistible modern spirituality, one that reveals the genius of Franciscan themes such as: simplicity, humility, joy, forgiveness, compassion, poverty, peacemaking, and care for creation.

ISBN 978-1-61636-859-3 | Hardcover with dust jacket | $22.99

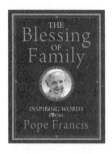

The Blessing of Family

"In the family, everything that enables us to grow, to mature and to live is given to each of us. We cannot grow up by ourselves, we cannot journey on our own, in isolation; rather, we journey and grow in a community, in a family."

—POPE FRANCIS, OCTOBER 9, 2013

Pope Francis cares deeply about the health and happiness not only of today's families, but also of tomorrow's families. The pope continues to keep the theme of the family in the forefront through his speeches, homilies, addresses, and writings. Published in cooperation with the Vatican, this original collection brings Pope Francis's teachings on the importance of family into focus in an elegant way. It covers themes of love and marriage, the promise of young people, and the vocation and mission of the family.

ISBN 978-1-61636-909-5 | Hardcover with dust jacket | $22.99

Pope Francis and Our Call to Joy

The essential guide to The Joy of the Gospel

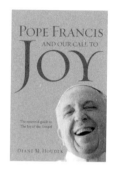

Pope Francis has set a new tone for the interaction between the church and the world, and that tone is one of joy, hope, and new life. Like his namesake, St. Francis of Assisi, he locates that joy in a personal encounter with Christ in the Gospels. By reflecting on his words and following his example, Christians can transform their own lives and relationships. *Pope Francis and Our Call to Joy* looks to discover the real Jesus in the Gospels, to understand the Church in the real world, to locate the special place of the poor and vulnerable and to find peace and the common good as part of our call in life.

ISBN 978-1-61636-849-4 | Paperback | $9.99

Order these books at your local bookstore, online, or direct from Franciscan Media by calling 1-888-322-6657.

ABOUT THE AUTHOR

Diane M. Houdek is digital editor at Franciscan Media and the author of *Lent with St. Francis, Advent with St. Francis,* and *Pope Francis and Our Call to Joy.*